HEALTHY ACTIVE LIVING
Student Activity Handbook 10

We are grateful to the following individuals for their contributions to this handbook:

Sheila Allen
Havergal College

Rasa Augaitis
St Mary's Catholic Secondary School

Sarah Bruce
Havergal College

Danielle Dutchak
Robert Bateman High School

Steve Friesen
St James Catholic School

Peter Glaab
St James Catholic School

Derek Graham
Westdale Secondary School

Dave Inglis
H B Beal Secondary School

Jamie Nunn
Vice-Principal, Westmount Secondary School

Kelly Pace
St. Clement's School

Kim Parkes
Westdale Secondary School

Kari Platman
Havergal College

Kelly Stenton
Havergal College

Carolyn Temertzoglou
Havergal College/Ontario Institute for Studies in Education (OISE)

Deb Townsley
North Middlesex District High School

Michele Van Bargen
Strathroy District Collegiate Institute

HEALTHY ACTIVE LIVING
Student Activity Handbook 10

Ted Temertzoglou

Birchmount Park Collegiate Institute
Toronto District School Board

Thompson Educational Publishing, Inc.
Toronto

Information on how to obtain copies of this book may be obtained from:

Website: www.thompsonbooks.com

E-mail: publisher@thompsonbooks.com

Telephone: (416) 766–2763

Fax: (416) 766–0398

ISBN: 978-1-55077-152-7

Credits:

PRELIMS: pp.13–15, courtesy of TDSB; pp. 17–19, with permission of A.Y. Jackson Secondary School (TDSB); pp. 21–23, photo by Michelle Prata. **UNIT 1:** p. 27, iStockphoto.com/Patrick1958; p. 30, artwork by Bart Vallecoccia; p. 31, with permission of Birchmount Park Collegiate Institute (TDSB); pp. 33–34, artwork by Bart Vallecoccia; p. 35, with permission of East York Collegiate Institute (TDSB); p. 36, with permission of A.Y. Jackson Secondary School (TDSB). **UNIT 2:** p. 37, photo by Michelle Prata; p. 39, with permission of Birchmount Park Collegiate Institute (TDSB); p. 40, with permission of Westwood Middle School (TDSB); pp. 44–46, photos by Ted Temertzoglou, Paul Pacey, and Tanya Winter ©Thompson Educational Publishing; p. 47, with permission of Birchmount Park Collegiate Institute (TDSB); p. 48, iStockphoto.com/Xonkdesign; p. 49, with permission of Birchmount Park Collegiate Institute (TDSB); p. 51, iStockphoto.com/sbayram. **UNIT 3:** p. 53, Mount Royal College Recreation Centre, Calgary, Alberta; p. 55, iStockphoto.com/walik; p. 58, photo by Ted Temertzoglou, Paul Pacey, and Tanya Winter ©Thompson Educational Publishing; pp. 60–61, with permission of Birchmount Park Collegiate Institute (TDSB). **UNIT 4:** p. 65, iStockphoto.com/Gurami; p. 73, iStockphoto.com/billnoll. **UNIT 5:** p. 75, iStockphoto.com/Catalinus; p. 82, iStockphoto.com/billnoll; p. 84, iStockphoto.com/kreativebrain. **UNIT 6:** p. 85, with permission of Birchmount Park Collegiate Institute (TDSB). **UNIT 7:** p. 93, iStockphoto.com/PIKSEL; p. 100, iStockphoto.com/Mr_Vector; p. 101, with permission of Birchmount Park Collegiate Institute (TDSB); p. 106, iStockphoto.com/billnoll. **UNIT 8:** pp. 109–110, courtesy of TDSB; pp. 111–112, with permission of Birchmount Park Collegiate Institute (TDSB); p. 113, with permission of Northern Secondary School (TDSB); p. 115, with permission of Birchmount Park Collegiate Institute (TDSB); p. 116, photo by Crystal J. Hall ©Thompson Educational Publishing.

Publisher: Keith Thompson

Managing editor: Jennie Worden

Cover design: Tibor Choleva

Page design, graphic art, and special effects: Tibor Choleva

Production editor: Crystal J. Hall

Copyeditor: Katy Harrison

Every reasonable effort has been made to acquire permission for copyrighted materials used in this book and to acknowledge such permissions accurately. Any errors or omissions called to the publisher's attention will be corrected in future printings. We acknowledge the support of the Government of Canada through the Book Publishing Industry Development Program for our publishing activities.

Printed in Canada.   2 3 4 5   09 08

Table of Contents

A Typical H&PE Class

You are about to rediscover the fascinating world of Health and Physical Education and the unique way in which it will enhance your life.

The health and physical education course is made up of four components: physical activity, active living, healthy living, and living skills. You will develop the necessary foundations to pursue a healthy active lifestyle and build a commitment to lifelong participation in health and physical activity.

Physical Activity & Active Living

In grade 9 you enjoyed regular participation in various physical activities, focusing on movement skills and principles, ways to improve physical fitness, and physical competence, all the while pursuing and promoting lifelong heathy active living goals. Grade 10 physical education is an expansion of these pursuits and commitments to healthy active living. You will learn the application of movement principles to hone your previously acquired skills and enhance your abilities in fitness. You will continue to partake in physical activities, demonstrate responsibility and knowledge for personal safety and the safety for your fellow classmates, as well as learn how to conduct a warm-up and lead a fitness activity.

Healthy Living & Living Skills

In grade 9 health you covered various issues from healthy sexuality; to the physical and psychological effects of the use and abuse of tobacco, alcohol, and illegal substances; to learning about conflict, anger management, the various forms of bullying and abuse, and communication skills. You will continue to investigate these issues in grade 10 health, with an emphasis on learning how to make informed decisions about sexual intimacy and relationships; the law and consequences pertaining to tobacco, alcohol, and substance use and abuse; conflict resolution through mediation and adjudication; and the foundations of nutrition, healthy eating habits, and the challenges faced with maintaining a healthy body image.

Remember that it is your effort, commitment, and determination to lead a healthy active lifestyle that remain the important factors in Health & Physical Education. The skills you learn are skills that can improve your quality of life throughout your lifetime.

Notes

Healthy Active Living

Assessing Your Participation

Category	Criteria	Level 1	Level 2	Level 3	Level 4
Participation	Demonstrates effort in activities and stays on task Is ready to participate and take part Demonstrates a determined effort	Infrequently participates actively	Sometimes participates actively	Regularly participates actively	Always or almost always participates actively
Safety	Demonstrates safe and correct procedures and use of equipment	Uses procedures and equipment safely and correctly only with supervision	Uses procedures and equipment safely and correctly with some supervision	Uses procedures and equipment safely and correctly	Demonstrates and promotes the correct use of procedures and equipment
Social	Demonstrates appropriate behaviour e.g., cooperation, respect, fair play, and works well with others	Infrequently demonstrates appropriate behaviour	Sometimes demonstrates appropriate behaviour	Regularly demonstrates appropriate behaviour	Always or almost always demonstrates appropriate behaviour

Okay, You Be the Teacher

This is your opportunity to be the teacher. Read the three case studies below and use the participation rubric on page 9 to assess these three students.

Case 1: Amar

Amar always comes to class prepared to participate. He is enthusiastic and he is never late. He appears eager to learn but he does not take direction well. Amar ignores the safety guidelines that are posted in the gymnasium and the weight-room. His actions jeopardize the safety of his fellow classmates as well as his personal safety.

Level _____ What advice would you offer Amar?

_____
_____
_____
_____
_____

Case 2: Cheryl

Cheryl tries hard in class. She arrives on time and prepared to participate. She helps out with set-up and cleanup. She reviews her activity journal and strives to maintain her fitness goals. She does show improvement but she is not athletically gifted. She works harder than most and enjoys being active.

Level _____ What advice would you offer Cheryl?

_____
_____
_____
_____
_____
_____

Case 3: Leland

Leland is on the basketball, and track and field teams. He also volunteers his time after school to assist the health & physical education department by scorekeeping for the girls basketball home games. He works hard practising for the teams he is involved with, but he lacks enthusiasm when he is in class. He often arrives late and tries to skip out early.

Level _____ What advice would you offer Leland?

_____
_____
_____
_____
_____

Using Your Daily Activity Journal

The Daily Activity Journal is a tool with which you should now be familiar. Monitoring your daily activity, both in school and out, is an excellent way to track your progress. In fact, successful people in many aspects of life do this on a regular basis. Below is a reminder on how to use the activity journal.

Mission: After each day, reflect on the physical activity you have engaged in and record it in your activity journal. If the activity was done during Health & Physical Education (H&PE) class, assess your participation, safety, and social skills. Refer to the rubric on page 9 for the criteria of each level. Be sure to use the symbols provided to describe your physical activity.

At the end of each month, you will have a very good snapshot of your monthly physical activity. Be sure to record your heart rate and total step count when appropriate.

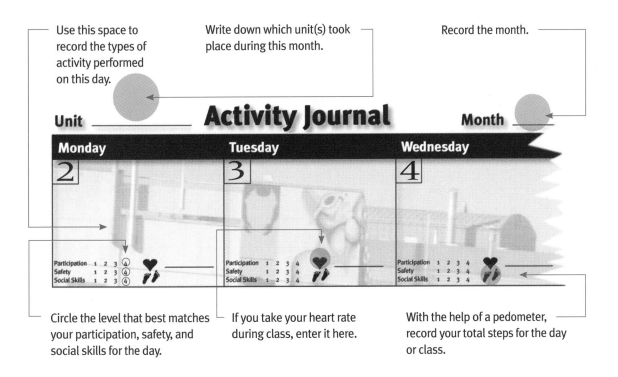

Use this space to record the types of activity performed on this day.

Write down which unit(s) took place during this month.

Record the month.

Circle the level that best matches your participation, safety, and social skills for the day.

If you take your heart rate during class, enter it here.

With the help of a pedometer, record your total steps for the day or class.

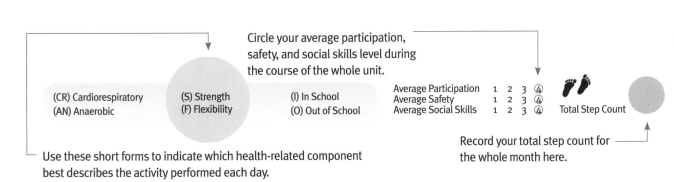

Circle your average participation, safety, and social skills level during the course of the whole unit.

(CR) Cardiorespiratory
(AN) Anaerobic

(S) Strength
(F) Flexibility

(I) In School
(O) Out of School

Use these short forms to indicate which health-related component best describes the activity performed each day.

Record your total step count for the whole month here.

Notes:

_____

_____

_____

_____

_____

_____

_____

_____

_____

_____

_____

_____

_____

_____

_____

_____

_____

_____

_____

_____

_____

_____

_____

_____

_____

_____

_____

Activity Journal

Unit _____ Month _____

Monday	Tuesday	Wednesday	Thursday	Friday
Participation 1 2 3 4 Safety 1 2 3 4 Social Skills 1 2 3 4	Participation 1 2 3 4 Safety 1 2 3 4 Social Skills 1 2 3 4	Participation 1 2 3 4 Safety 1 2 3 4 Social Skills 1 2 3 4	Participation 1 2 3 4 Safety 1 2 3 4 Social Skills 1 2 3 4	Participation 1 2 3 4 Safety 1 2 3 4 Social Skills 1 2 3 4
Participation 1 2 3 4 Safety 1 2 3 4 Social Skills 1 2 3 4	Participation 1 2 3 4 Safety 1 2 3 4 Social Skills 1 2 3 4	Participation 1 2 3 4 Safety 1 2 3 4 Social Skills 1 2 3 4	Participation 1 2 3 4 Safety 1 2 3 4 Social Skills 1 2 3 4	Participation 1 2 3 4 Safety 1 2 3 4 Social Skills 1 2 3 4
Participation 1 2 3 4 Safety 1 2 3 4 Social Skills 1 2 3 4	Participation 1 2 3 4 Safety 1 2 3 4 Social Skills 1 2 3 4	Participation 1 2 3 4 Safety 1 2 3 4 Social Skills 1 2 3 4	Participation 1 2 3 4 Safety 1 2 3 4 Social Skills 1 2 3 4	Participation 1 2 3 4 Safety 1 2 3 4 Social Skills 1 2 3 4

(CR) Cardiorespiratory (S) Strength (I) In School
(AN) Anaerobic (F) Flexibility (O) Out of School

Average Participation 1 2 3 4
Average Safety 1 2 3 4
Average Social Skills 1 2 3 4

Total Step Count _____

Activity Journal

Unit _____ Month _____

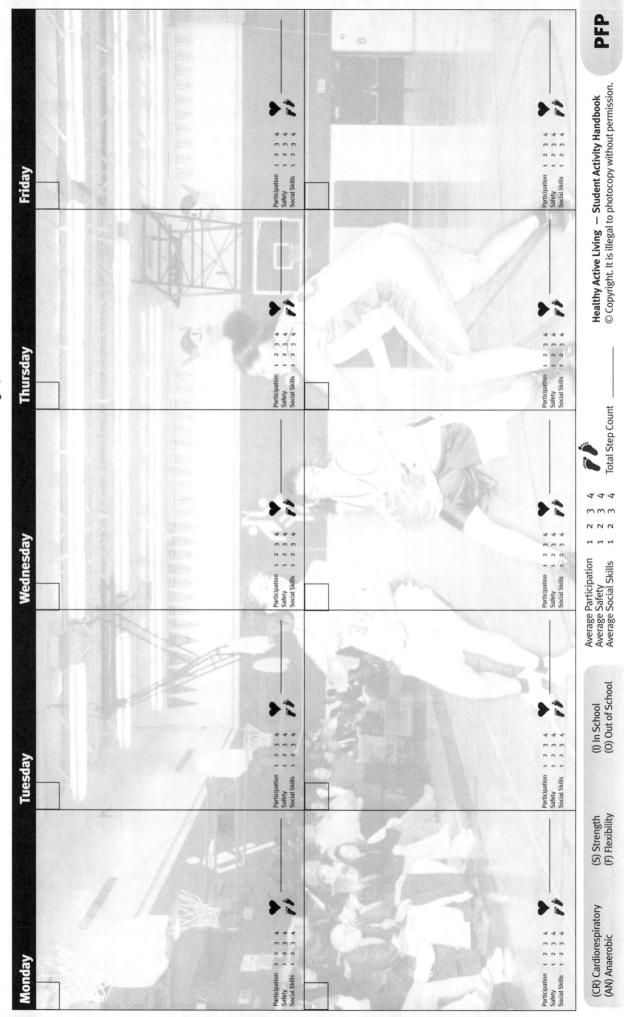

Monday	Tuesday	Wednesday	Thursday	Friday

Participation 1 2 3 4
Safety 1 2 3 4
Social Skills 1 2 3 4

Participation 1 2 3 4
Safety 1 2 3 4
Social Skills 1 2 3 4

Participation 1 2 3 4
Safety 1 2 3 4
Social Skills 1 2 3 4

Participation 1 2 3 4
Safety 1 2 3 4
Social Skills 1 2 3 4

Participation 1 2 3 4
Safety 1 2 3 4
Social Skills 1 2 3 4

Participation 1 2 3 4
Safety 1 2 3 4
Social Skills 1 2 3 4

Participation 1 2 3 4
Safety 1 2 3 4
Social Skills 1 2 3 4

Participation 1 2 3 4
Safety 1 2 3 4
Social Skills 1 2 3 4

Participation 1 2 3 4
Safety 1 2 3 4
Social Skills 1 2 3 4

Participation 1 2 3 4
Safety 1 2 3 4
Social Skills 1 2 3 4

(CR) Cardiorespiratory
(AN) Anaerobic

(S) Strength
(F) Flexibility

(I) In School
(O) Out of School

Average Participation 1 2 3 4
Average Safety 1 2 3 4
Average Social Skills 1 2 3 4

Total Step Count _____

Weekend Activities

Month _____

Saturday—(Week 1)	Sunday—(Week 1)
♥ _____ 👣	♥ _____ 👣
Saturday—(Week 2)	Sunday—(Week 2)
♥ _____ 👣	♥ _____ 👣
Saturday—(Week 3)	Sunday—(Week 3)
♥ _____ 👣	♥ _____ 👣
Saturday—(Week 4)	Sunday—(Week 4)
♥ _____ 👣	♥ _____ 👣

👣 Total Step Count _____

Average Participation	1	2	3 4
Average Safety	1	2	3 4
Average Social Skills	1	2	3 4

(I) In School   (S) Strength
(O) Out of School   (F) Flexibility

(CR) Cardiorespiratory
(AN) Anaerobic

Activity Journal Questions

Once you have finished your monthly recordings, complete the sentence stems below.

1. The one area of fitness I improved upon the most was ...

_____

_____

Rationale: _____

2. An area of fitness I can improve on is ...

_____

_____

Rationale: _____

3. Something I found challenging during this unit(s) was ...

_____

_____

Rationale: _____

4. During this unit(s), I was most proud of myself when ...

_____

_____

Rationale: _____

5. Reflecting back on this unit(s), I would give myself the following levels based on my participation, safety practices, and social skills (refer to page 9 to review the criteria for each level):

Participation: Level _____   I gave myself this level because:

_____

Safety: Level _____   I gave myself this level because:

_____

Social: Level _____   I gave myself this level because:

_____

PFP

Activity Journal

Unit _____ Month _____

Monday	Tuesday	Wednesday	Thursday	Friday

Monday

Participation 1 2 3 4
Safety 1 2 3 4
Social Skills 1 2 3 4

Participation 1 2 3 4
Safety 1 2 3 4
Social Skills 1 2 3 4

Participation 1 2 3 4
Safety 1 2 3 4
Social Skills 1 2 3 4

Tuesday

Participation 1 2 3 4
Safety 1 2 3 4
Social Skills 1 2 3 4

Participation 1 2 3 4
Safety 1 2 3 4
Social Skills 1 2 3 4

Participation 1 2 3 4
Safety 1 2 3 4
Social Skills 1 2 3 4

Wednesday

Participation 1 2 3 4
Safety 1 2 3 4
Social Skills 1 2 3 4

Participation 1 2 3 4
Safety 1 2 3 4
Social Skills 1 2 3 4

Participation 1 2 3 4
Safety 1 2 3 4
Social Skills 1 2 3 4

Thursday

Participation 1 2 3 4
Safety 1 2 3 4
Social Skills 1 2 3 4

Participation 1 2 3 4
Safety 1 2 3 4
Social Skills 1 2 3 4

Participation 1 2 3 4
Safety 1 2 3 4
Social Skills 1 2 3 4

Friday

Participation 1 2 3 4
Safety 1 2 3 4
Social Skills 1 2 3 4

Participation 1 2 3 4
Safety 1 2 3 4
Social Skills 1 2 3 4

Participation 1 2 3 4
Safety 1 2 3 4
Social Skills 1 2 3 4

(CR) Cardiorespiratory
(AN) Anaerobic

(S) Strength
(F) Flexibility

(I) In School
(O) Out of School

Average Participation 1 2 3 4
Average Safety 1 2 3 4
Average Social Skills 1 2 3 4

Total Step Count _____

Healthy Active Living — Student Activity Handbook

PFP

Activity Journal   Month ____

Unit ____

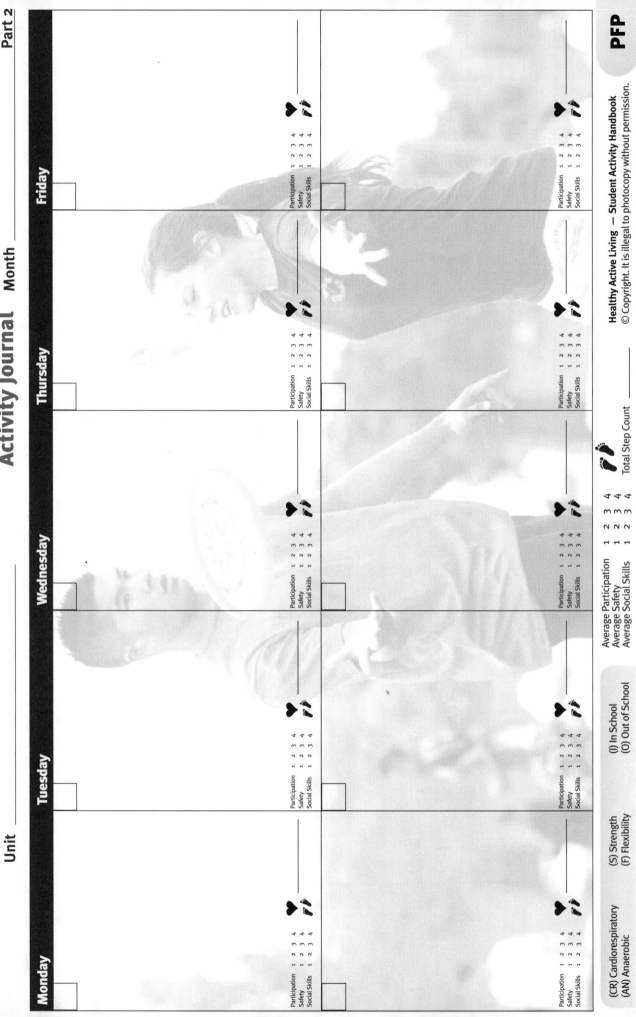

Monday	Tuesday	Wednesday	Thursday	Friday

Participation 1 2 3 4
Safety   1 2 3 4
Social Skills 1 2 3 4

Participation 1 2 3 4
Safety   1 2 3 4
Social Skills 1 2 3 4

Participation 1 2 3 4
Safety   1 2 3 4
Social Skills 1 2 3 4

Participation 1 2 3 4
Safety   1 2 3 4
Social Skills 1 2 3 4

Participation 1 2 3 4
Safety   1 2 3 4
Social Skills 1 2 3 4

Participation 1 2 3 4
Safety   1 2 3 4
Social Skills 1 2 3 4

Participation 1 2 3 4
Safety   1 2 3 4
Social Skills 1 2 3 4

Participation 1 2 3 4
Safety   1 2 3 4
Social Skills 1 2 3 4

(CR) Cardiorespiratory
(AN) Anaerobic

(S) Strength
(F) Flexibility

(I) In School
(O) Out of School

Average Participation 1 2 3 4
Average Safety   1 2 3 4
Average Social Skills 1 2 3 4

Total Step Count ____

Healthy Active Living — Student Activity Handbook

PFP

Weekend Activities

Month _____

Saturday — (Week 1)	**Sunday — (Week 1)**
♥ _____	♥ _____

Saturday — (Week 2)	**Sunday — (Week 2)**
♥ _____	♥ _____

Saturday — (Week 3)	**Sunday — (Week 3)**
♥ _____	♥ _____

Saturday — (Week 4)	**Sunday — (Week 4)**
♥ _____	♥ _____

	1	2	3	4	Total Step Count _____
Average Participation	1	2	3	4	
Average Safety	1	2	3	4	
Average Social Skills	1	2	3	4	

(I) In School
(O) Out of School

(S) Strength
(F) Flexibility

(CR) Cardiorespiratory
(AN) Anaerobic

Activity Journal Questions

Once you have finished your monthly recordings, complete the sentence stems below.

1. The one area of fitness I improved upon the most was ...

_____

_____

Rationale: _____

2. An area of fitness I can improve on is ...

_____

_____

Rationale: _____

3. Something I found challenging during this unit(s) was ...

_____

_____

Rationale: _____

4. During this unit(s), I was most proud of myself when ...

_____

_____

Rationale: _____

5. Reflecting back on this unit(s), I would give myself the following levels based on my participation, safety practices, and social skills (refer to page 9 to review the criteria for each level):

Participation: Level _____   I gave myself this level because:

_____

Safety: Level _____   I gave myself this level because:

_____

Social: Level _____   I gave myself this level because:

_____

PFP

Activity Journal

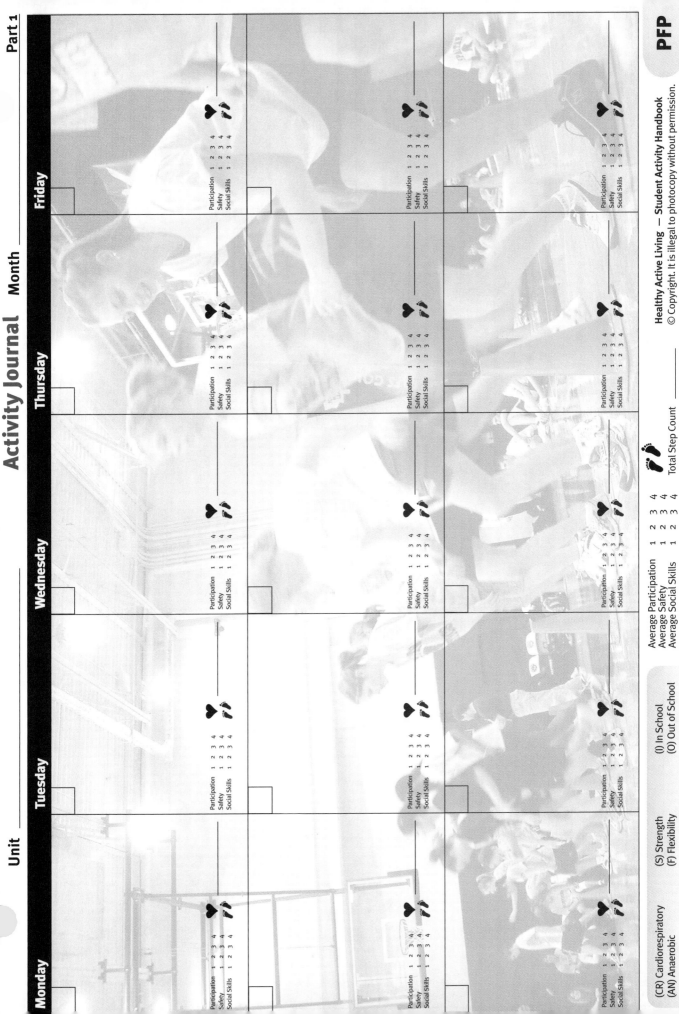

	Monday	Tuesday	Wednesday	Thursday	Friday
Row 1	Participation 1 2 3 4 Safety 1 2 3 4 Social Skills 1 2 3 4	Participation 1 2 3 4 Safety 1 2 3 4 Social Skills 1 2 3 4	Participation 1 2 3 4 Safety 1 2 3 4 Social Skills 1 2 3 4	Participation 1 2 3 4 Safety 1 2 3 4 Social Skills 1 2 3 4	Participation 1 2 3 4 Safety 1 2 3 4 Social Skills 1 2 3 4
Row 2	Participation 1 2 3 4 Safety 1 2 3 4 Social Skills 1 2 3 4	Participation 1 2 3 4 Safety 1 2 3 4 Social Skills 1 2 3 4	Participation 1 2 3 4 Safety 1 2 3 4 Social Skills 1 2 3 4	Participation 1 2 3 4 Safety 1 2 3 4 Social Skills 1 2 3 4	Participation 1 2 3 4 Safety 1 2 3 4 Social Skills 1 2 3 4
Row 3	Participation 1 2 3 4 Safety 1 2 3 4 Social Skills 1 2 3 4	Participation 1 2 3 4 Safety 1 2 3 4 Social Skills 1 2 3 4	Participation 1 2 3 4 Safety 1 2 3 4 Social Skills 1 2 3 4	Participation 1 2 3 4 Safety 1 2 3 4 Social Skills 1 2 3 4	Participation 1 2 3 4 Safety 1 2 3 4 Social Skills 1 2 3 4

(CR) Cardiorespiratory   (S) Strength   (I) In School   Average Participation 1 2 3 4   Total Step Count _____
(AN) Anaerobic   (F) Flexibility   (O) Out of School   Average Safety 1 2 3 4
Average Social Skills 1 2 3 4

PFP

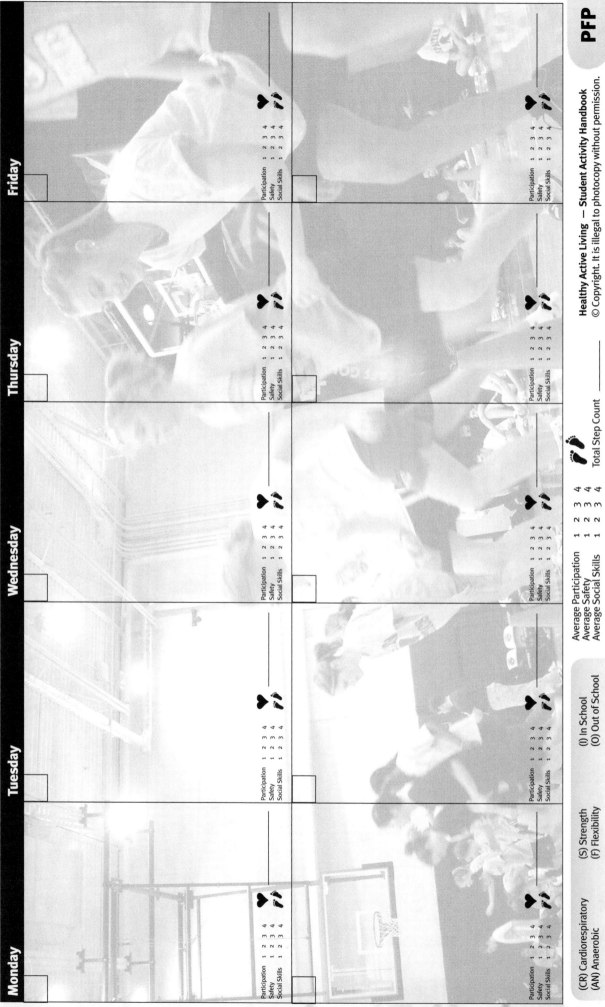

Activity Journal

Unit _____   Month _____

Monday	Tuesday	Wednesday	Thursday	Friday

Participation 1 2 3 4
Safety 1 2 3 4
Social Skills 1 2 3 4

(CR) Cardiorespiratory (S) Strength (I) In School
(AN) Anaerobic (F) Flexibility (O) Out of School

Average Participation 1 2 3 4
Average Safety 1 2 3 4
Average Social Skills 1 2 3 4
Total Step Count

Weekend Activities

Month _____

Saturday—(Week 1)	Sunday—(Week 1)
♥ _____	♥ _____

Saturday—(Week 2)	Sunday—(Week 2)
♥ _____	♥ _____

Saturday—(Week 3)	Sunday—(Week 3)
♥ _____	♥ _____

Saturday—(Week 4)	Sunday—(Week 4)
♥ _____	♥ _____

Total Step Count

Average Participation	1	2	3	4
Average Safety	1	2	3	4
Average Social Skills	1	2	3	4

(I) In School
(O) Out of School

(S) Strength
(F) Flexibility

(CR) Cardiorespiratory
(AN) Anaerobic

Activity Journal Questions

Once you have finished your monthly recordings, complete the sentence stems below.

1. The one area of fitness I improved upon the most was …

_____

_____

Rationale: _____

2. An area of fitness I can improve on is …

_____

_____

Rationale: _____

3. Something I found challenging during this unit(s) was …

_____

_____

Rationale: _____

4. During this unit(s), I was most proud of myself when …

_____

_____

Rationale: _____

5. Reflecting back on this unit(s), I would give myself the following levels based on my participation, safety practices, and social skills (refer to page 9 to review the criteria for each level):

Participation: Level _____ I gave myself this level because:

_____

Safety: Level _____ I gave myself this level because:

_____

Social: Level _____ I gave myself this level because:

_____

PFP

The *Healthy Active Living* Scavenger Hunt

Now is your chance to put your detective skills to work. This "scavenger hunt" will help you become familiar with the features and information in your *Healthy Active Living* textbook.

Mission: Use your textbook to find the answers to the following questions.

1. Using the Table of Contents, find the chapter number for Body Image and Self-Esteem: How do you see yourself?

2. Where in the textbook will you find the Myths and Facts about Drugs?

3. Where in the textbook is the table that lists Various Styles of Dance?

4. Using the Table of Contents, find the name for chapter 9.

5. Where in the textbook will you find a listing of all the Key Terms?

6. List the four subtitles in the Defining Your Limits: Practise Your Communication Skills box found in chapter 12.

7. Where in the textbook will you find the Warm-Up and Cool-Down Exercises?

8. Where in the textbook will you find the table on Common Vegetarian Eating Styles?

9. Find the chapter that covers Wrestling/Combative Sports.

10. Where in the textbook will you find A Guide to Action?

11. Where in the textbook will you find the Dot Drill Standards for Girls and Boys?

12. What graph appears on page 3 of the textbook?

13. Where in the textbook will you find the table on Immediate, Short-Term, and Long-Term Effects of Marijuana Use?

14. Where in the textbook will you find the SHARP and PIER: Identifying and Treating Injuries box?

15. What graph appears on page 169 of the textbook?

Year at a Glance

Mission: Use the following calendar to record your units, assessments, evaluation dates, and any other important dates for your H&PE course.

September					
Monday	Tuesday	Wednesday	Thursday	Friday	Saturday/Sunday

February					
Monday	Tuesday	Wednesday	Thursday	Friday	Saturday/Sunday

October					
Monday	Tuesday	Wednesday	Thursday	Friday	Saturday/Sunday

March					
Monday	Tuesday	Wednesday	Thursday	Friday	Saturday/Sunday

November					
Monday	Tuesday	Wednesday	Thursday	Friday	Saturday/Sunday

April					
Monday	Tuesday	Wednesday	Thursday	Friday	Saturday/Sunday

December					
Monday	Tuesday	Wednesday	Thursday	Friday	Saturday/Sunday

May					
Monday	Tuesday	Wednesday	Thursday	Friday	Saturday/Sunday

January					
Monday	Tuesday	Wednesday	Thursday	Friday	Saturday/Sunday

June					
Monday	Tuesday	Wednesday	Thursday	Friday	Saturday/Sunday

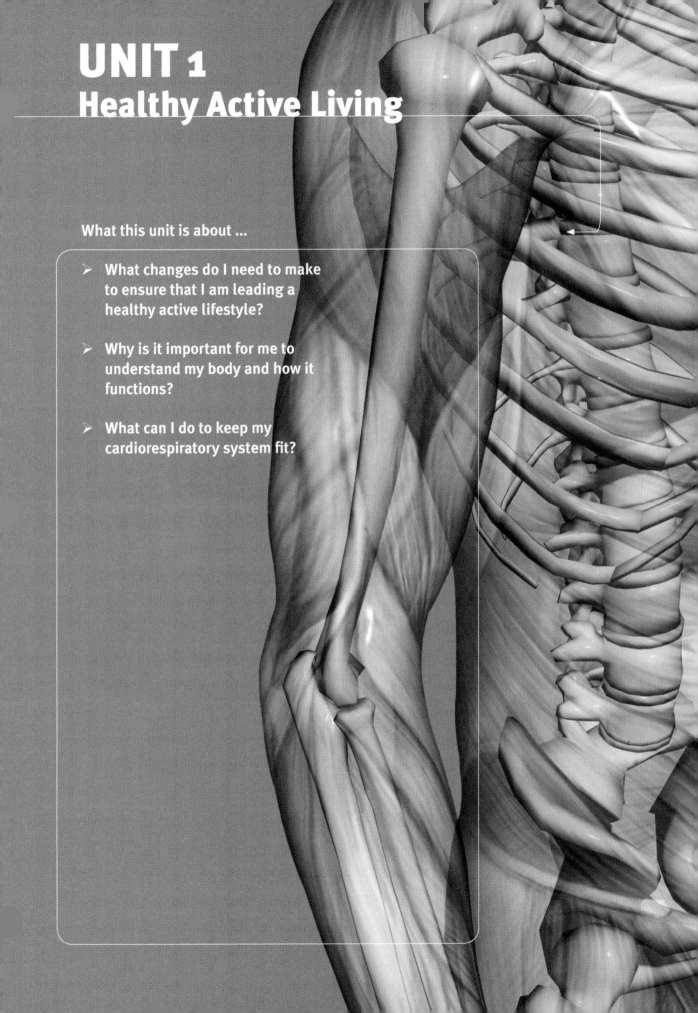

UNIT 1
Healthy Active Living

What this unit is about ...

➤ **What changes do I need to make to ensure that I am leading a healthy active lifestyle?**

➤ **Why is it important for me to understand my body and how it functions?**

➤ **What can I do to keep my cardiorespiratory system fit?**

Notes

Exercise 1.1

Four Components of Healthy Active Living

The following exercises should be completed without the use of your textbook.

Mission: There are four components to healthy active living: physical health, mental health, social health, and spiritual health. Provide a definition for each of the four components and give three examples that support why achieving good physical, mental, social, and spiritual health is important.

Good physical health means:

_____

_____

Three examples are:

_____

_____

_____

Good mental health means:

_____

_____

Three examples are:

_____

_____

_____

Healthy Active Living

Good social health means:

_____

_____

Three examples are:

_____

_____

_____

Good spiritual health means:

_____

_____

Three examples are:

_____

_____

_____

PFP

Types of Bones: Mix and Match

Mission: Complete the following table by matching the numbered diagrams to the terms on the left-hand side of the page. Provide an example (other than the illustrated example) of where in your body each type of bone can be found.

Type of bone	#	Location in body
Long bone		
Flat bone		
Irregular bone		
Sesamoid bone		
Short bone		

Healthy Heart and Lungs: Key Terms

Mission: Place the terms below into the sentence that best describes their meaning.

artery   blood pressure   aerobic system   adenosine triphosphate (ATP)   lactic acid

1. The _____ allows us to perform over longer periods of time at a fairly balanced intensity.

2. _____ is a substance that builds up inside the muscle fibres and can cause extreme pain.

3. An _____ carries blood away from the heart.

4. _____ refers to the force exerted by the blood against the walls of the artery

5. The energy we use to move around takes the form of an "energy molecule" called _____.

Exercise 1.2

Anatomical Axes & Planes

Look in the Book
Pages: 20–21

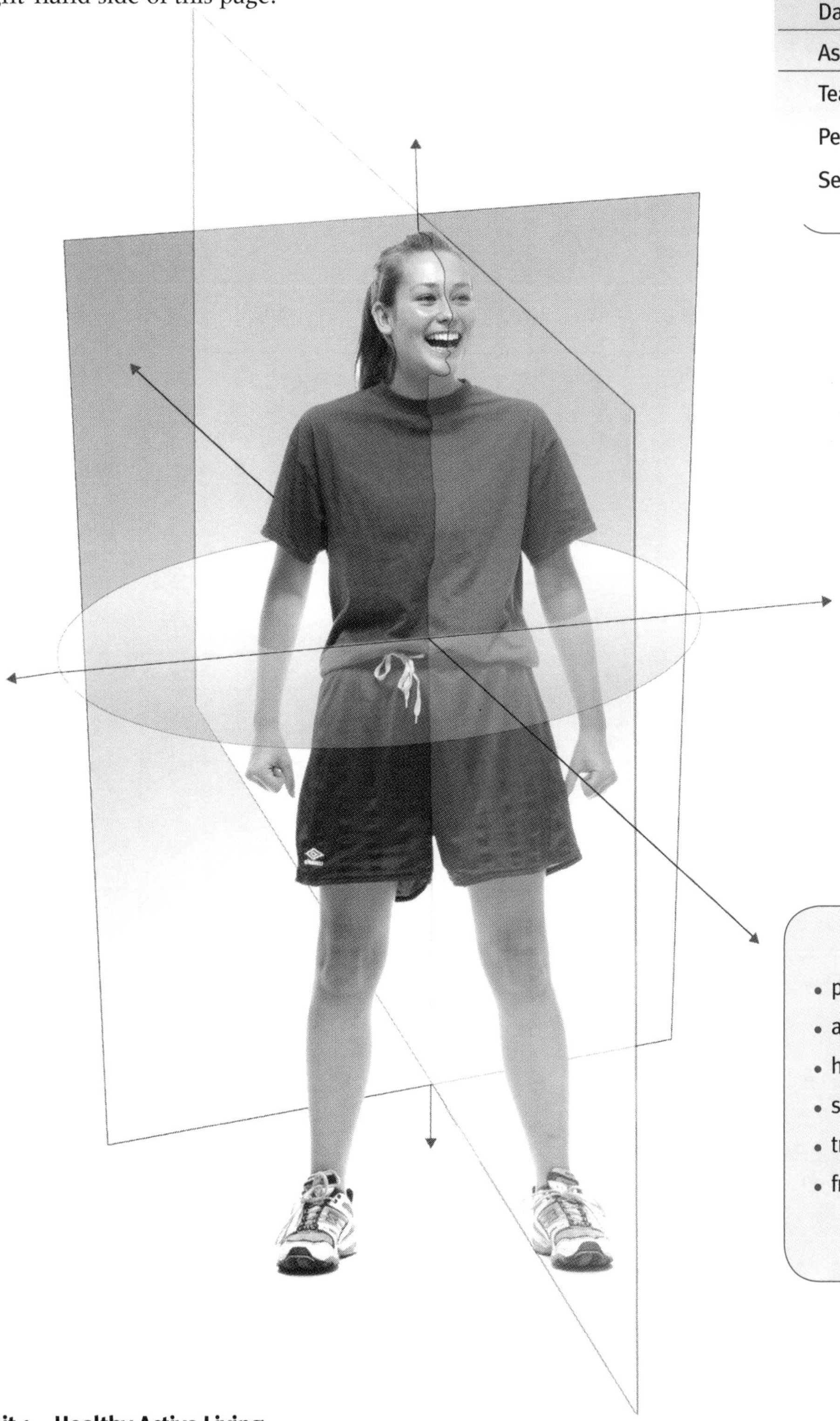

Student name:	
Class/Period:	
Date:	
Assessed by:	
Teacher	☐
Peer	☐
Self	☐

Anatomical axes and planes are the imaginary lines and flat planes that are used to describe movement.

Mission: Label the anatomical axes and planes using the terms on the right-hand side of this page.

- polar axis
- anteroposterior axis
- horizontal axis
- sagittal plane
- transverse plane
- frontal plane

The Relationship Between Axes and Planes

Axes and planes are always at right angles to each other. Remembering this rule can make describing position and movement much easier.

Mission: Describe the form of movement occurring in the examples provided below, by filling in the axis of rotation in relation to the plane of movement.

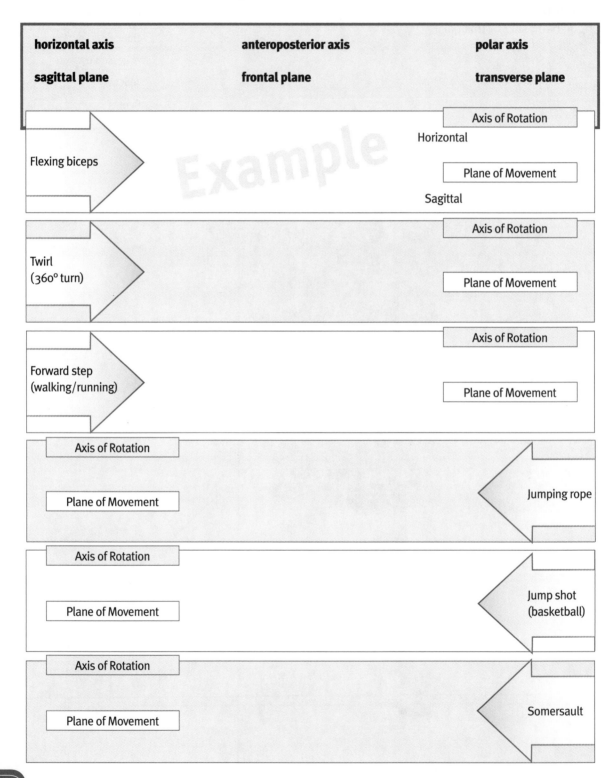

horizontal axis	anteroposterior axis	polar axis
sagittal plane	frontal plane	transverse plane

Flexing biceps

Axis of Rotation
Horizontal

Plane of Movement
Sagittal

Twirl (360° turn)

Axis of Rotation

Plane of Movement

Forward step (walking/running)

Axis of Rotation

Plane of Movement

Jumping rope

Axis of Rotation

Plane of Movement

Jump shot (basketball)

Axis of Rotation

Plane of Movement

Somersault

Axis of Rotation

Plane of Movement

Exercise 1.3

The Synovial Joint

Look in the Book
Pages: 33–35

Synovial joints provide the most movement and are the most common of all joints found in the body.

Mission: Use a different coloured pencil crayon to colour each word on the right-hand side of the page. Then use the same colour to identify the corresponding part of the synovial joint below.

Student name:

Class/Period:

Date:

Assessed by:

Teacher ☐

Peer ☐

Self ☐

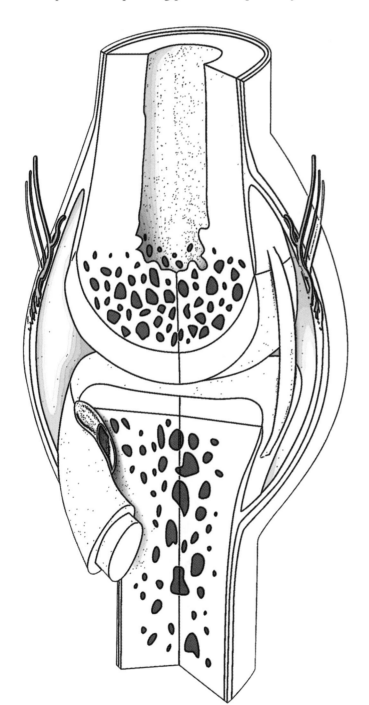

☐ Periosteum
☐ Joint cavity
☐ Joint capsule
☐ Tendons
☐ Bone
☐ Blood vessels
☐ Nerves
☐ Bursae
☐ Ligaments
☐ Articular cartilage

Types of Synovial Joints

There are six types of synovial joints. Some types allow for limited movement (one direction), while others allow for maximal movement (multi-direction).

Mission: Name each type of synovial joint and describe the type of movement each synovial joint allows.

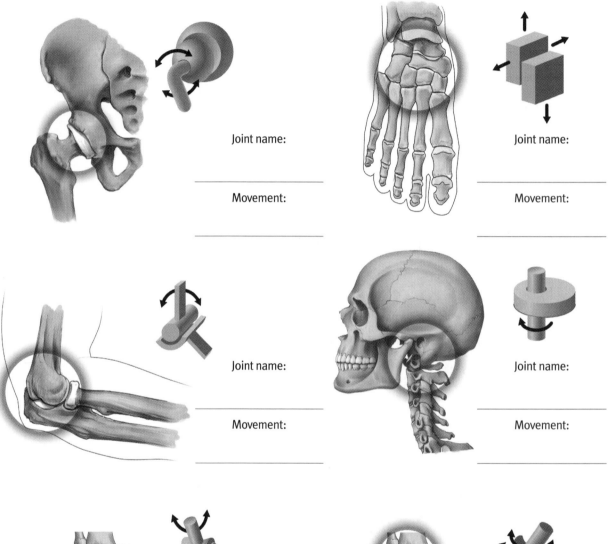

Joint name:

_____

Movement:

_____

Joint name:

_____

Movement:

_____

Joint name:

_____

Movement:

_____

Joint name:

_____

Movement:

_____

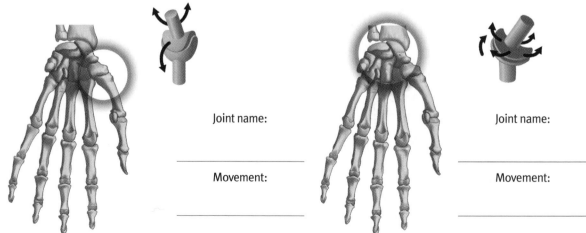

Joint name:

_____

Movement:

_____

Joint name:

_____

Movement:

_____

Exercise 1.4

Health-Related Fitness

Look in the Book
Pages: 8–11

Health-related fitness is generally assessed in five main areas: cardiorespiratory, muscular strength, muscular endurance, flexibility, and body composition.

Mission: Indicate, with a check mark, one or more of the health-related components emphasized in each of the sports/activities listed below.

Student name:

Class/Period:

Date:

Assessed by:

Teacher ☐

Peer ☐

Self ☐

SPORT/ACTIVITY	CARDIORESPIRATORY	MUSCULAR STRENGTH	MUSCULAR ENDURANCE	FLEXIBILITY
Soccer	☐	☐	☐	☐
Basketball	☐	☐	☐	☐
Canadian Football	☐	☐	☐	☐
Volleyball	☐	☐	☐	☐
Tennis	☐	☐	☐	☐
Baseball/ Softball	☐	☐	☐	☐
Golf	☐	☐	☐	☐
Track and Field	☐	☐	☐	☐
Gymnastics	☐	☐	☐	☐
Dance	☐	☐	☐	☐
Skiing	☐	☐	☐	☐

Skill-Related Fitness

Skill-related fitness centres on the following six components: agility, balance, coordination, power, reaction time, and speed.

Mission: Indicate with a check mark, one or more of the skill-related components emphasized in each of the sports/activities listed below.

SPORT/ACTIVITY	AGILITY	BALANCE	COORDINATION	POWER	REACTION TIME	SPEED
Ultimate Frisbee	☐	☐	☐	☐	☐	☐
Field Hockey	☐	☐	☐	☐	☐	☐
Lacrosse	☐	☐	☐	☐	☐	☐
Badminton	☐	☐	☐	☐	☐	☐
Table Tennis	☐	☐	☐	☐	☐	☐
Cricket	☐	☐	☐	☐	☐	☐
Curling	☐	☐	☐	☐	☐	☐
Wrestling/Combatives	☐	☐	☐	☐	☐	☐
Aquatics	☐	☐	☐	☐	☐	☐
Yoga and Pilates	☐	☐	☐	☐	☐	☐
Orienteering	☐	☐	☐	☐	☐	☐

UNIT 2
Fitness Measurements and Appraisals

What this unit is about ...

➢ Why is it important for me always to stay within my Target Heart Rate Zone when I am involved in various physical activities?

➢ What is musculoskeletal fitness, and why is it important for me to partake in musculoskeletal appraisals?

➢ How can assessing my body composition help me to understand my fitness needs?

Fitness Appraisal Tracking Sheet

Based on how you did last year and how you think you may do this year, fill out a personal fitness continuum to help you gain a firm understanding of your physical health, and determine what areas you are strongest in versus what areas you may need to improve upon.

Mission: Before you partake in the fitness appraisals, predict how well you will do by drawing a line along the "Prediction" row. Then, once you have completed the fitness appraisals, draw a line along the "Actual" row that reflects how well you did. Answer the questions that follow.

Cardiorespiratory Appraisals

PERCEPTION	Low	Moderate	High
PREDICTION			
ACTUAL			

Muscular Strength and Endurance Appraisals

PERCEPTION	Low	Moderate	High
PREDICTION			
ACTUAL			

Performance-Level Appraisals

PERCEPTION	Low	Moderate	High
PREDICTION			
ACTUAL			

On which appraisal(s) was your prediction the most accurate? _____

_____

Rationale: _____

_____

_____

On which appraisal(s) was your prediction the least accurate? _____

_____

Rationale: _____

_____

_____

PFP

Exercise 2.1

Activate Prior Knowledge

Look in the Book
Pages: 62–69, 73–85

This exercise will help you and your teacher identify what you know, what you want to know, and what you have learned about fitness appraisals.

Mission: Complete the "K" column with all the details you **know** about personal fitness appraisals. Record any questions you **want** answered about personal fitness appraisals in the "W" column. Read about the personal fitness appraisals in your *Healthy Active Living* textbook, and after you have performed them, record any new information that you have **learned** in the "L" column.

Student name:

Class/Period:

Date:

Assessed by:

Teacher ☐

Peer ☐

Self ☐

KWL FOR PERSONAL FITNESS APPRAISALS		
K	**W**	**L**
What do I KNOW?	What do I WANT to know?	What have I LEARNED?

PFP

Your Target Heart Rate Zone

Look in the Book
Pages: 59–61

To achieve significant improvements in the health of your cardiorespiratory system, you must stay within your **Target Heart Rate Zone** when exercising. To find your Target Heart Rate Zone, follow the four steps below.

Step 1: Resting Heart Rate

Find your Resting Heart Rate (RHR) by placing your index and middle finger on your carotid artery (on your neck) when you are not engaged in physical activity. Count the "pulses" against your fingers for 10 seconds and complete the formula below:

Heart rate after 10 sec. _____ × 6 = RHR of _____ beats per minute (bpm).

Step 2: Maximal Heart Rate

Find your Maximal Heart Rate (MHR) by subtracting your age from 220:

220 bpm – your age = _____ MHR

Step 3: Heart Rate Reserve

Find your Heart Rate Reserve (HRR) by subtracting your RHR from your MHR:

MHR _____ – RHR _____ = _____ HRR

Step 4: Target Heart Rate Zone

Multiply your HRR by .5 (to find the lower limit) and then by .85 (to find the upper limit). Then add the result to your RHR to find your Target Heart Rate Zone.

Lower limit of your Target Heart Rate Zone (50%)

HRR _____ × .5 (50%) = _____ + RHR _____ = _____

Upper limit of your Target Heart Rate Zone (85%)

HRR _____ × .85 (85%) = _____ + RHR _____ = _____

Has your Target Heart Rate Zone remained the same since grade 9?
_____

Rationale: _____
_____
_____
_____

PFP

Exercise 2.3

Cardiorespiratory Appraisals

Cardiorespiratory appraisals gauge the efficiency of your heart and lungs and provide you with an indication of your overall fitness. With the help of your teacher, choose a cardiorespiratory appraisal that best suits your current level of fitness. If there are medical reasons why you cannot participate, notify your teacher immediately.

PART 1: mCAFT

Part A: Before You Begin

Using the sidebar on page 64 of your *Healthy Active Living* textbook, find your Starting Stage and Ceiling Heart Rate and record them below.

Starting stage _____

Ceiling Heart Rate count: _____ 10-second count in beats per minute

_____ for heart rate monitor in beats per minute

Part B: Ready Set Go!

Should you reach or surpass the Ceiling Heart Rate for your age at any time during the appraisal, you must immediately stop.

Record your final heart rate and the final stage you achieved in the space provided below.

Final Heart Rate _____ bpm

Final stage achieved _____

Part C: Record Your Progress

Record your appraisal date and colour the stage level you achieved in the graph provided.

HEALTH BENEFIT ZONES FOR FITNESS	
Excellent	Your fitness falls within a range that is generally associated with optimal health benefits.
Very Good	Your fitness falls within a range that is generally associated with considerable health benefits.
Good	Your fitness falls within a range that is generally associated with many health benefits.
Fair	Your fitness falls within a range that is generally associated with some health risks.
Needs Improvement	Your fitness falls within a range that is generally associated with considerable health risks.

The large arrow indicates the zone where improvements represent the greatest gains to your health.

Stages

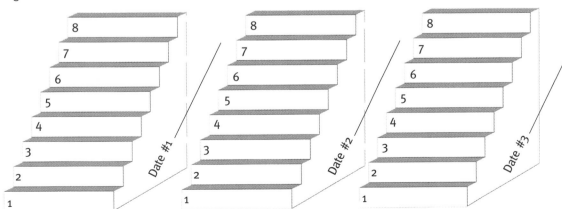

PART 2: 12–Minute Run

This appraisal is suitable for all fitness levels, but make sure you are properly warmed up before you try the appraisal. Once the appraisal begins, jog or run at a steady pace, and try to remain running for the duration of the appraisal. If you need to walk at anytime then do so.

Number of laps or metres completed after 12 minutes _____

Best score last year:_____ Best score this year:_____

After each appraisal, record the number of laps covered in the appropriate lane below. Use the sidebar on the top right-hand corner to convert your laps into kilometres.

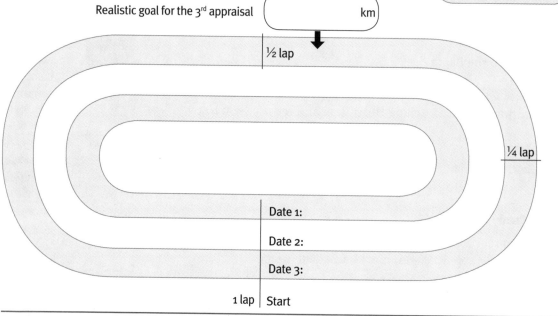

Realistic goal for the 3rd appraisal [_____ km]

½ lap

¼ lap

Date 1:
Date 2:
Date 3:

1 lap | Start

PART 3: Beep Test

This is one of the most accurate tests in determining your current cardiorespiratory fitness level. It is a "maximal" appraisal, which means you will be going all out. You should only attempt this test if you are in good physical condition and only under the supervision of qualified instructors. If you would like to view your results against the Beep Test Standards, refer to page 69 of your *Healthy Active Living* textbook.

Best score last year:_____
Best score this year:_____

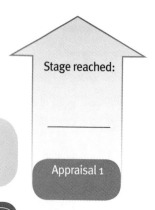

Stage reached:

_____

Appraisal 1

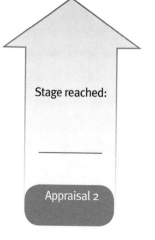

Stage reached:

_____

Appraisal 2

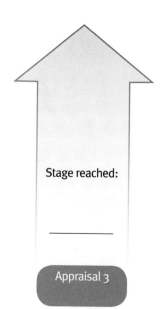

Stage reached:

_____

Appraisal 3

PFP

Exercise 2.3

Unit 2—Fitness Measurements and Appraisals

Exercise 2.4

Muscular Strength and Endurance Appraisals

These appraisals measure overall musculoskeletal fitness: muscular strength, muscular endurance, and the flexibility of your joints.

PART 1: Grip Strength

This appraisal measures the strength of your forearm muscles.

Mission: For each appraisal date, write down the results of your two separate attempts for both your left hand and your right hand in the spaces provided. Add the two maximum scores together and record the total in the box at the top of the dynamometers.

Best score last year: _____   Best score this year: _____

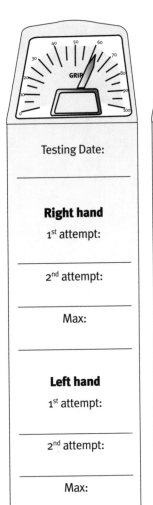

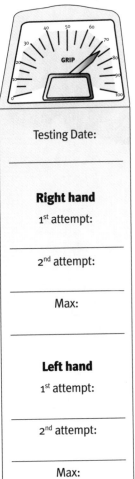

HEALTH BENEFIT ZONES FOR FITNESS	
Excellent	Your fitness falls within a range that is generally associated with optimal health benefits.
Very Good	Your fitness falls within a range that is generally associated with considerable health benefits.
Good	Your fitness falls within a range that is generally associated with many health benefits.
Fair	Your fitness falls within a range that is generally associated with some health risks.
Needs Improvement	Your fitness falls within a range that is generally associated with considerable health risks.

The large arrow indicates the zone where improvements represent the greatest gains to your health.

Testing Date: _____

Right hand

1st attempt: _____

2nd attempt: _____

Max: _____

Left hand

1st attempt: _____

2nd attempt: _____

Max: _____

Testing Date: _____

Right hand

1st attempt: _____

2nd attempt: _____

Max: _____

Left hand

1st attempt: _____

2nd attempt: _____

Max: _____

Testing Date: _____

Right hand

1st attempt: _____

2nd attempt: _____

Max: _____

Left hand

1st attempt: _____

2nd attempt: _____

Max: _____

PFP

PART 2: Push-Ups

The push-up appraisal measures muscular endurance, and is a good all-around indicator of upper-body strength.

Mission: Record the date of each appraisal and the total number of push-ups you were able to perform in the spaces below.

Best score last year:_____ Best score this year:_____

Date
_____

1. _____

Date
_____

2. _____

Date
_____

3. _____

PFP

44

Exercise 2.4

Unit 2 — Fitness Measurements and Appraisals

PART 3: Partial Curl-Up

The partial curl-up appraisal measures the muscular strength and endurance of the abdominal muscles.

Mission: Record the date of each appraisal and the total number of partial curl-ups you were able to perform in the spaces below.

Best score last year:_____   Best score this year:_____

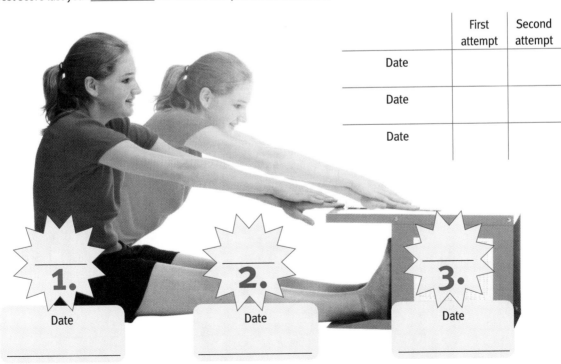

3.
Date
_____

1.
Date
_____

2.
Date
_____

PART 4: Sit-and-Reach

The Sit-and-Reach appraisal measures joint flexibility using a special device called a flexometer.

Mission: For each appraisal date, write down the results of your two separate attempts in the spaces provided. Then, record your best results in spaces below.

Best score last year:_____ Best score this year:_____

	First attempt	Second attempt
Date		
Date		
Date		

1.
Date
_____

2.
Date
_____

3.
Date
_____

PFP

PART 5: Vertical Jump

The Vertical Jump Appraisal measures muscular power and requires the use of almost all the major muscles in the body.

Mission: For each appraisal date, write down the results of your two separate attempts in the arrows on the right-hand side of the page. Then, record your best result from each appraisal date in spaces below.

Best score last year:_____   Best score this year:_____

HEALTH BENEFIT ZONES FOR FITNESS

Excellent	Your fitness falls within a range that is generally associated with optimal health benefits.
Very Good	Your fitness falls within a range that is generally associated with considerable health benefits.
Good	Your fitness falls within a range that is generally associated with many health benefits.
Fair	Your fitness falls within a range that is generally associated with some health risks.
Needs Improvement	Your fitness falls within a range that is generally associated with considerable health risks.

The large arrow indicates the zone where improvements represent the greatest gains to your health.

PFP

305 cm
(Height + Vertical)

3.	**Date**	First attempt	Second attempt

2.	**Date**	First attempt	Second attempt

1.	**Date**	First attempt	Second attempt

Unit 2—Fitness Measurements and Appraisals

Exercise 2.5

Performance-Level Appraisals

Student name: _____

Class/Period: _____

Date: _____

Assessed by: _____

Teacher ☐

Peer ☐

Self ☐

Performance-level appraisals focus on specific movement skills such as, speed, agility, and coordination. They are intended for measuring and improving particular aspects of performance as opposed to overall health.

PART 1: Dot Drill

The Dot Drill is an appraisal that assesses quickness, agility, and muscular endurance.

Mission: Record the date of each appraisal and the time (in seconds) that it took you to complete the five patterns—don't forget to repeat all five patterns six times consecutively. If you wish to compare your results to the standards, refer to page 81 in your *Healthy Active Living* textbook.

1ˢᵗ appraisal   Date _____   Time _____ sec

2ⁿᵈ appraisal   Date _____   Time _____ sec

3ʳᵈ appraisal   Date _____   Time _____ sec

PART 2: Illinois Agility Run

The Illinois Agility Run is a good appraisal to use to assess your ability to change direction quickly and accurately without the loss of balance.

Mission: Record the date of each appraisal and the time (in seconds) that it took you to complete the course.

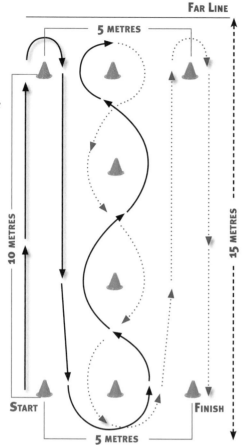

FAR LINE

5 METRES

10 METRES

15 METRES

5 METRES

START

FINISH

1st appraisal
Date

_____

Time: _____ sec

2nd appraisal
Date

_____

Time: _____ sec

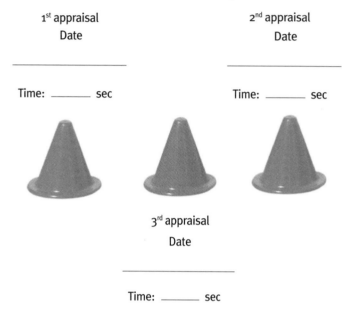

3rd appraisal
Date

_____

Time: _____ sec

PART 3: Wall-Ball Toss

The Wall-Ball Toss measures hand-eye coordination, a skill that is important in games such as tennis, baseball, and lacrosse.

Mission: Record the date of each appraisal and the number of successful catches that did not hit the floor.

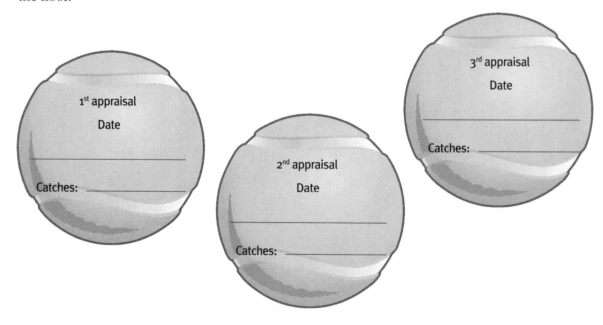

1st appraisal
Date

_____

Catches: _____

2nd appraisal
Date

_____

Catches: _____

3rd appraisal
Date

_____

Catches: _____

PART 4: 20-Yard and 40-Yard Sprints

The 20- and 40-Yard Sprint is a good appraisal to assess your ability to accelerate quickly.

Mission: For each appraisal date, write down your times (in seconds) from the start line to the 20-yard mark and the 40-yard mark. If you wish to compare your results to the standards, refer to page 84 in your *Healthy Active Living* textbook.

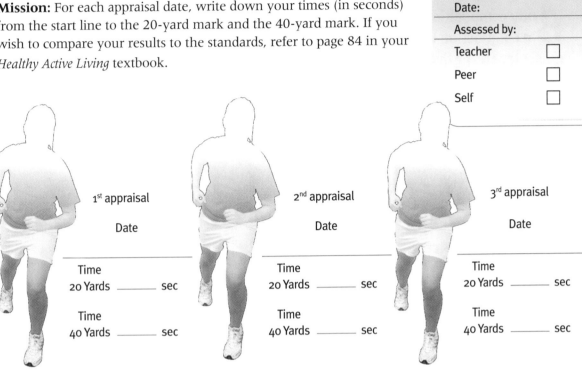

1st appraisal

Date _____

Time
20 Yards _____ sec

Time
40 Yards _____ sec

2nd appraisal

Date _____

Time
20 Yards _____ sec

Time
40 Yards _____ sec

3rd appraisal

Date _____

Time
20 Yards _____ sec

Time
40 Yards _____ sec

PART 5: Chin-Ups and Flexed-Arm Hang

The Chin-Ups and Flexed-Arm Hang Appraisals measure muscular strength and endurance of the forearms, arms, and shoulders.

Mission: With the guidance of your instructor, choose the appraisal that best suits your level of muscular strength and endurance. Record the date of each appraisal and either the number of chin-ups you were able to perform for the chin-ups appraisal, or the time (in seconds) you were able to hold the position for the flexed-arm hang appraisal.

Chin-Ups

1st appraisal   Date _____   # of chin-ups _____

2nd appraisal   Date _____   # of chin-ups _____

3rd appraisal   Date _____   # of chin-ups _____

Flexed-Arm Hang

1st appraisal   Date _____   Time _____ sec

2nd appraisal   Date _____   Time _____ sec

3rd appraisal   Date _____   Time _____ sec

Body Composition Appraisals

Look in the Book
Pages: 90 & 92

Body composition appraisals need to be used in conjunction with the cardiorespiratory and muscular strength and endurance appraisals. Combined, these three types of appraisals will provide a fairly accurate assessment of your fitness needs.

Student name: _____

Class/Period: _____

Date: _____

Assessed by: _____

Teacher ☐

Peer ☐

Self ☐

PART 1: BMI

The Body Mass Index (BMI) provides a rough indication as to whether your body weight (mass) is appropriate for your height.

Mission: To determine your BMI, follow the steps listed on page 90 in your *Healthy Active Living* textbook. Record your results in the equation below.

$$BMI = \frac{\underline{\hspace{2cm}} \, kg}{m^2} = $$

PART 2: Waist Circumference

The Waist Circumference (WC) appraisal is effective in predicting the health risks that come with excess fat weight around your midsection.

Mission: To determine your WC value, follow the steps listed on page 92 in your *Healthy Active Living* textbook. Record your measurement in the space provided below.

WC= _____ cm

PART 3: WC + BMI

Though widely used, the BMI does not distinguish between body fat and dense muscle, nor does it take into account where the fat resides. To achieve a better indication of your body composition, combine your BMI with your Waist Circumference (WC). Refer to the table on page 92 in your *Healthy Active Living* textbook to determine your overall body composition rating and record it in the space provided below.

Overall body composition rating: _____

Exercise 2.7

Lead a Fitness Activity

Student name: _____

Class/Period: _____

Date: _____

Assessed by: _____

Teacher ☐

Peer ☐

Self ☐

When choosing an activity to help you stay fit, you should look for one that improves your muscular strength, muscular endurance, and flexibility, and assists in building your cardiorespiratory fitness.

Mission: With the fitness knowledge that you have already acquired, devise a fitness activity that the entire class can enjoy.

Activity: _____

Duration of Activity: _____

Equipment/materials for the participants:

_____

_____

_____

_____

Equipment/materials for the facilitator (you):

_____

_____

_____

_____

_____

Rules (outline your activity using step-by-step instructions):

❶ _____

❷ _____

❸ _____

❹ _____

❺ _____

Diagram of Gym/Field Setup:

Where are you? Where are the participants?

1. Explain why you chose this particular activity: _____

_____

_____

2. Are you happy with the results of the activity? _____

Rationale: _____

_____

3. What would you do differently next time? _____

Rationale: _____

_____

UNIT 3
Fitness Planning, Exercises, and Injury Prevention

What this unit is about ...

➤ Why should I set fitness goals for myself, and how can I make those goals a reality?

➤ Why will knowing and understanding how my major muscles work help me to exercise them in the best way possible?

➤ What does exercise safety mean to me, and why is it important that I follow the appropriate safety measures when involved in various physical activities?

Notes:

_____

_____

_____

_____

_____

_____

_____

_____

_____

_____

_____

_____

_____

_____

_____

_____

_____

_____

_____

_____

_____

_____

_____

_____

_____

_____

_____

_____

Exercise 3.1

My Healthy Active Living Profile

Now that you have completed your fitness measurements and appraisals for a second year, your next step is to set clear, realistic goals to help you achieve your desired outcomes.

Mission: Review your goals from last year and build upon them using the SMART and action plans.

In grade 9, my Healthy Active Living goal was:

_____

I would like to improve upon My Healthy Active Living goal by:

_____

_____

Student name:

_____

Class/Period:

_____

Date:

Assessed by:

Teacher ☐

Peer ☐

Self ☐

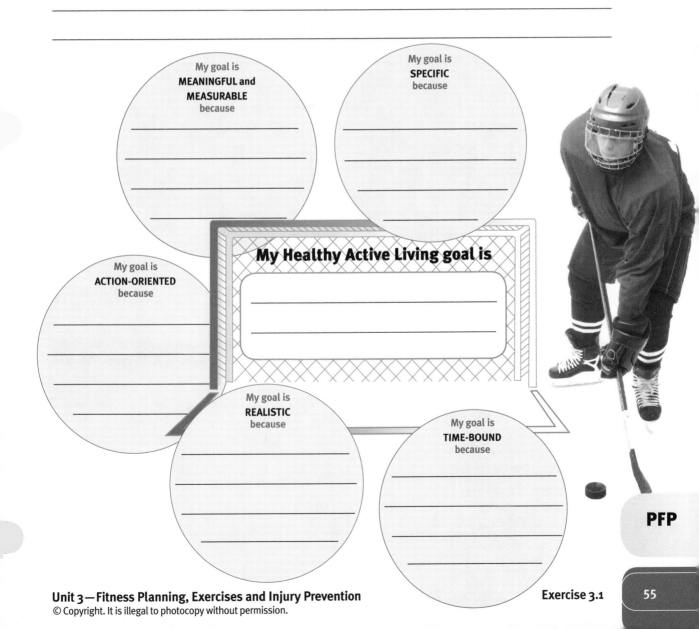

My goal is
MEANINGFUL and MEASURABLE
because

_____
_____
_____

My goal is
SPECIFIC
because

_____
_____
_____

My goal is
ACTION-ORIENTED
because

_____
_____
_____

My Healthy Active Living goal is

_____
_____

My goal is
REALISTIC
because

_____
_____
_____

My goal is
TIME-BOUND
because

_____
_____
_____

PFP

What special skills or knowledge do I have to help me achieve this goal?

Skills:	Knowledge:
_____	_____
_____	_____
_____	_____

Action steps to take:

Today I will: _____

_____

By next week I will: _____

_____

By next month, I will: _____

_____

By the end of the school year, I will: _____

_____

	THINKING ABOUT IT	BEGINNING	WELL UNDERWAY	DONE!
I created realistic goals for my fitness level.				
I worked on achieving my goals on a regular basis.				
I reassessed my goals and made the appropriate changes.				
I'm comfortable in setting fitness goals. I can follow the SMART formula throughout my life.				
I feel that I've achieved a level of fitness that is healthy for me.				

PFP

The FITT Principle

Date:
Pages: 106–107

FITT refers to the four elements that any good training plan should include: Frequency, Intensity, Time (or duration), and Type of activity.

Mission: Use this chart to outline your overall fitness program. Keep in mind all four elements to help you maintain and/or improve your current fitness level.

Student name:

Class/Period:

Date:

FITT	CARDIORESPIRATORY	FLEXIBILITY	MUSCULAR ENDURANCE	MUSCULAR STRENGTH
F Frequency				
I Intensity				
T Time				
T Type of activity				

PFP

Exercises for Fitness and Health

There are hundreds of exercises you can do to improve your fitness and health. The following five target specific muscles and/or muscle groups.

Mission: Identify the following five exercises and name the muscle or muscle group each exercise targets by using the terms listed on the bottom left-hand card.

Name of the exercise

Muscle or Muscle Group

Name of the exercise

Muscle or Muscle Group

Name of the exercise

Muscle or Muscle Group

Exercises
- Stability Ball Concentration Curls
- Triceps Kickbacks
- Bird Dog
- Single-Leg Squats
- Single-Leg Calf Raises

Muscle/Muscle Groups
- Quadriceps
- Biceps
- Gastrocnemius
- Triceps
- Erector Spinae Group

Name of the exercise

Muscle or Muscle Group

Name of the exercise

Muscle or Muscle Group

Unit 3—Fitness Planning, Exercises and Injury Prevention

Exercise 3.3

Lead the Warm-Up

Before participating in any type of physical activity, it is important to warm up the body. A warm-up will improve muscle elasticity, lubricate the joints, and prepare tendons and ligaments for physical activity.

Mission: Devise a warm-up that the entire class can perform. Remember to include light aerobic activity and dynamic stretching.

Aerobic Activity

Duration

I chose this activity because: _____

_____

1st dynamic stretch:

I chose this stretch because: _____

_____

2nd dynamic stretch:

I chose this stretch because: _____

_____

3rd dynamic stretch:

I chose this stretch because: _____

_____

Injury Prevention and Safety

Look in the Book
Page: 149

Participating in any sport or physical activity can present a level of risk; therefore, you must be safety conscious at all times. It is not enough that you remain aware of proper technique; you must also abide by the safety guidelines and rules to ensure both your own safety, and that of your classmates.

Mission: View the photo of the weight room below. Find and circle the ten different dangers/safety hazards. Then, in the space provided below the photo, describe what you should do to fix each situation.

1. _____

2. _____

3. _____

4. _____

5. _____

6. _____

7. _____

8. _____

9. _____

10. _____

Exercise 3.4

Where Do I Go From Here?

This exercise should be completed at the end of the semester/term as a reflection on what you have achieved, and the successes and/or challenges you may have faced while trying to reach your fitness goals.

Mission: Complete the following worksheet as a way of reflecting on your experience in H&PE.

1. How were you encouraged to achieve your fitness goals?

- _____
- _____
- _____
- _____

2. How were you supported in trying to achieve your fitness goals?

- _____
- _____
- _____
- _____

3. What discouraged you in trying to achieve your fitness goals?

- _____
- _____
- _____
- _____

PFP

4. What did you learn about yourself while trying to reach your fitness goals?

- _____
- _____
- _____
- _____

5. What did you learn about decision making in achieving your fitness goals?

- _____
- _____
- _____
- _____

6. What did you learn that you will use in the future?

- _____
- _____
- _____
- _____

7. What have you learned about fitness and its importance to your daily life?

- _____
- _____
- _____
- _____

PFP

Unit 3—Fitness Planning, Exercises and Injury Prevention

Resistance Training Log

The weight you train with need not be excessive in order for you to benefit from resistance training. As long as you use moderate weights and closely follow your instructor's directions, you can make resistance training a valuable part of your fitness plan.

Mission: With the help of your instructor, fill in the exercises you wish to do during your resistance training unit. Record the starting weight, tempo, and number of repetitions you perform in each set (as instructed by your teacher) in the spaces provided.

Exercise	Starting Weight	Tempo	Set 1	Set 2	Set 3	Rest

Resistance Training Log

Exercise	Starting Weight	Tempo	Set 1	Set 2	Set 3	Rest

Unit 3—Fitness Planning, Exercises and Injury Prevention

UNIT 4
Human Reproduction, Sexuality, and Intimacy

What this unit is about ...

➢ Why is it important for me to take good care of my reproductive system?

➢ What is sexual development, and how do I know if mine is normal?

➢ How can I make good decisions about sexuality and intimacy?

Notes:

_____

_____

_____

_____

_____

_____

_____

_____

_____

_____

_____

_____

_____

_____

_____

_____

_____

_____

_____

_____

_____

_____

_____

_____

_____

_____

_____

_____

_____

_____

_____

Unit 4—Sexuality, Human Reproduction and Intimacy

Exercise 4.1

What Do I Know About Human Reproduction?

The following exercises should be completed without the use of your textbook.

Mission: Read each statement and decide whether you think they are "True" or "False."

❶ The female reproductive system is responsible only for carrying and delivering babies. | TRUE ☐ | FALSE ☐

Rationale:

❷ The vagina connects with the uterus at the cervix. | TRUE ☐ | FALSE ☐

Rationale:

❸ Monilia is caused by the yeast fungus *Candida albicans*. | TRUE ☐ | FALSE ☐

Rationale:

❹ All ovarian cysts are cancerous. | TRUE ☐ | FALSE ☐

Rationale:

❺ The male reproductive system is responsible only for producing, nourishing, and transporting sperm. | TRUE ☐ | FALSE ☐

Rationale:

❻ Semen is produced from the three accessory glands. | TRUE ☐ | FALSE ☐

Rationale:

❼ A hernia is a painful condition that requires minor surgery. | TRUE ☐ | FALSE ☐

Rationale:

❽ Testicular cancer is the most common problem associated with the male reproductive system. | TRUE ☐ | FALSE ☐

Rationale:

❾ All women should perform a monthly breast self-examination (BSE) seven to ten days after the start of their periods. | TRUE ☐ | FALSE ☐

Rationale:

❿ A testicular self-examination (TSE) can be performed by your physician only. | TRUE ☐ | FALSE ☐

Rationale:

Sexuality and Intimacy: Key Terms

Every day, we are all exposed to information about sex and sexuality and confronted with choices about relationships and sexual decision making. In order to make good decisions about sex, you need a fundamental understanding of what sexuality and intimacy entails.

Mission: Place the terms below into the sentence that best describes their meaning.

sexuality   heterosexual   self-esteem   homosexual

healthy relationships   sexual intimacy   socialization

transgender   gender   methods of contraception

1. In _____, partners respect themselves and one another; and consider and show concern for each other's feelings.

2. _____ encompasses our physical development, sexual knowledge, attitudes, values, and behaviours. In other words, it includes everything that defines us as girls and boys, women and men.

3. Someone who is _____ feels sexual attraction towards people of the same sex.

4. _____ is a way of expressing intimate feelings for another person.

5. The term _____ applies to social factors; it is the condition of being female or male as defined by society.

6. Enforced by family, peers, and school, _____ is a process that continues throughout an individual's lifetime.

7. _____ is a feeling of pride in yourself and a sense of self-worth.

8. People who identify as _____ may choose to dress and present themselves as members of the opposite sex without undergoing Sexual Reassignment Surgery.

9. _____ are designed to impede the union of the sperm and egg and prevent pregnancy.

10. Someone who is _____ feels an exclusive sexual attraction toward people of the opposite sex.

Exercise 4.2

Influences on Sexuality

It is difficult for individuals to find a clear sense of sexuality when faced with so many inaccurate messages and contradictions.

Mission: Identify one potential influence on sexuality for each page in the brochure below and list what impact each factor may have on an individual's sexuality. Then, use a five-star rating (with five stars being very influential) to indicate the degree to which each factor influences *your* sexuality.

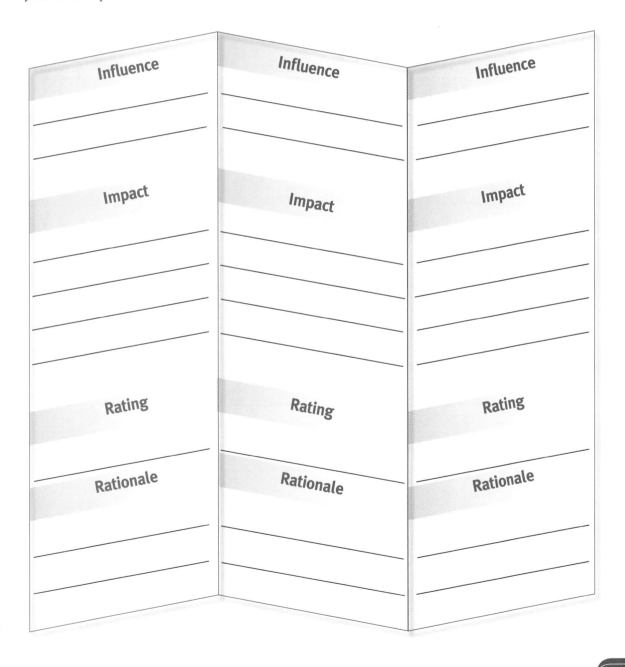

Sex as a Sales Tool

The media often uses stereotypical notions of femininity or masculinity to tell us what is appropriate and desirable for women and men.

Mission: Select a magazine advertisement that shows a female and a male together. Analyze the advertisement by filling out the table below.

Advertisement: _____

Target Audience: _____

FACTORS TO CONSIDER	FEMALE	MALE
APPEARANCE: What do they look like (thin, tall, tanned, blonde, etc.)?		
CLOTHING: What are they wearing (casual clothes, underwear, swimsuit, etc.)?		
FEELINGS: What expressions are they making (smiling, laughing, solemn, etc.)?		
POSITION: What is their position in relation to each other (holding hands, leaning in, hugging, etc.)?		

After taking the above factors into consideration, do you think the advertisement makes suggestions of a sexual nature? - - - - - - - - - - ▶

Rationale: _____

_____

_____

Do you think this advertisement will have an impact on the sexuality of the target audience? - - - - - - - - - - - - - - - - - - - ▶

Rationale: _____

_____

_____

Exercise 4.3

Decision Making—IDEAL in Action

Look in the Book
Page: xix

It is up to you to consider the possible consequences of the choices that you make about sexual intimacy, and what level of intimacy is acceptable to you.

Mission: Using the IDEAL model below, create a scenario that involves a decision about sexual intimacy and identify a basic problem/concern. Outline options for dealing with the situation, and evaluate the pros and cons of each choice. Once you arrive at a decision, explain why you made that choice and what you learned from the experience.

Student name:

Class/Period:

Date:

Assessed by:

Teacher ☐

Peer ☐

Self ☐

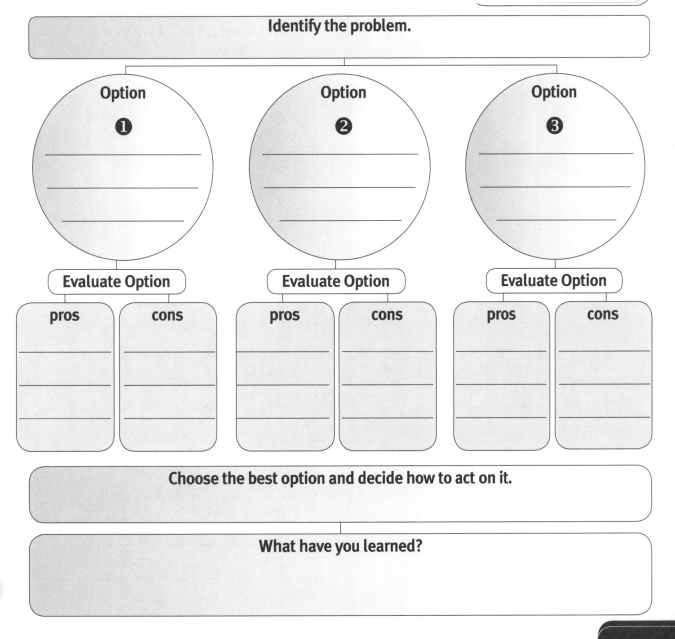

Identify the problem.

Option ❶

Option ❷

Option ❸

Evaluate Option
pros | cons

Evaluate Option
pros | cons

Evaluate Option
pros | cons

Choose the best option and decide how to act on it.

What have you learned?

Sexual Intimacy

The pace at which a couple moves through the steps of sexual intimacy will depend on a wide variety of factors; but all decisions about sex and sexuality need to be made with all of the possible consequences in mind.

Mission: Read the case studies below and answer the questions that follow.

Case Study #1:

Mark and Danuta have been dating since grade 9 and are now in their final year of high school. They may attend different universities. This concerns them both. Mark feels that they should have sexual intercourse as a means of securing their relationship whereas Danuta wants to wait until marriage, which is what they had agreed upon. Mark pressures Danuta and, in fear of losing Mark, she reluctantly gives in. They choose not to use any form of protection because they are both virgins and therefore feel that there is nothing they need to protect against.

Case Study #2:

Cathy is a virgin. Jerome, her boyfriend of several months, is pressuring Cathy to have sexual intercourse with him. She refuses, believing it is too soon to engage in sexual intercourse because she is only fifteen. Jerome argues that he would like to express his affection for her in a more physical manner, but Cathy feels comfortable with their current level of intimacy. Jerome asks Cathy if she would be willing to try some activities that are less intimate than intercourse. Cathy thinks about his offer, but decides against it.

1. What steps in the decision-making process did the couples take in order to make their decisions?

_____

_____

2. Highlight the emotional or physical health concerns that arose from their decisions and list contact information for support services that cater to their specific concerns.

_____

_____

3. Provide your opinion about the decisions that were made. Consider whether everyone's needs were respected and whether the choices made were responsible and safe?

_____

_____

Unit 4—Sexuality, Human Reproduction and Intimacy

Exercise 4.4

Information & Support Services

Adolescence is a time during which individuals are faced with many physical, emotional, and social changes as they make the transition from childhood to adulthood. It can be an overwhelming and sometimes confusing time.

Mission: Using the spaces below, identify services available in your community for people needing advice on, or help with, sexual decision making, contraception, or other matters related to sexuality.

Finding Help—Where to Go With Questions

Support service:

Services provided:

Contact information:

Support service:

Services provided:

Contact information:

Make It Known

Using various media is a great way to inform adolescents of where they can go to get help with questions about sexuality, or other matters related to sexuality.

Mission: Using the space provided below, create an awareness advertisement for one of the two support services you researched. You can draw, paint, or create a collage advertising the support service, write a television commercial, or design a pamphlet. Be sure to include the name of the service and the contact information.

UNIT 5
Drug Use and Abuse

What this unit is about ...

➢ Why do some people use harmful drugs and what are the possible health consequences?

➢ What are the short- and long-term health effects of tobacco and alcohol on the body?

➢ What are the illegal drugs and what options are available for those who have become dependent on them?

Notes:

_____

_____

_____

_____

_____

_____

_____

_____

_____

_____

_____

_____

_____

_____

_____

_____

_____

_____

_____

_____

_____

_____

_____

_____

_____

_____

_____

_____

_____

Unit 5—Drug Use and Abuse

Exercise 5.1

What Do I Know About Drugs?

Student name:

Class/Period:

Date:

Assessed by:

Teacher ☐

Peer ☐

Self ☐

The following exercises should be completed without the use of your textbook.

Mission: Read the following statements and indicate whether you think each statement is "True" or "False."

---

❶ Psychoactive drugs affect our mental and emotional state. | TRUE ☐ | FALSE ☐

Rationale:

---

❷ The continuum of drug use is a way of measuring your potential drug use and the risks associated with it. | TRUE ☐ | FALSE ☐

Rationale:

---

❸ Bingeing is a safe practice for drug or alcohol intake. | TRUE ☐ | FALSE ☐

Rationale:

---

❹ Smoking causes over 21 percent of all deaths in Canada each year. | TRUE ☐ | FALSE ☐

Rationale:

---

❺ The amount of alcohol in the breath is not related to the amount of alcohol in the blood. | TRUE ☐ | FALSE ☐

Rationale:

---

❻ Overuse of alcohol can lead to ulcers, inflammation, and bleeding of the stomach and intestines. | TRUE ☐ | FALSE ☐

Rationale:

---

❼ Liquor control regulations govern the sale and advertisement of alcohol. | TRUE ☐ | FALSE ☐

Rationale:

---

❽ The Gateway Theory proposes that someone who uses marijuana will not go on to use drugs such as cocaine and heroin. | TRUE ☐ | FALSE ☐

Rationale:

---

❾ Rohypnol®, GHB, and Ketamine are commonly considered date rape drugs. | TRUE ☐ | FALSE ☐

Rationale:

---

❿ "Roids," "juice," "gym candy," "pumpers," and "stackers" are common or street names for Anabolic Steroids. | TRUE ☐ | FALSE ☐

Rationale:

The Continuum of Drug Use

Drug use for non-medical reasons almost always poses a degree of risk. The continuum of drug use is a way of measuring potential drug use and the degree of risk and harm associated with it.

Mission: There are different levels of drug use, and each of these has a certain level of risk that accompanies it. List some of the risks associated with each level in the appropriate spaces below.

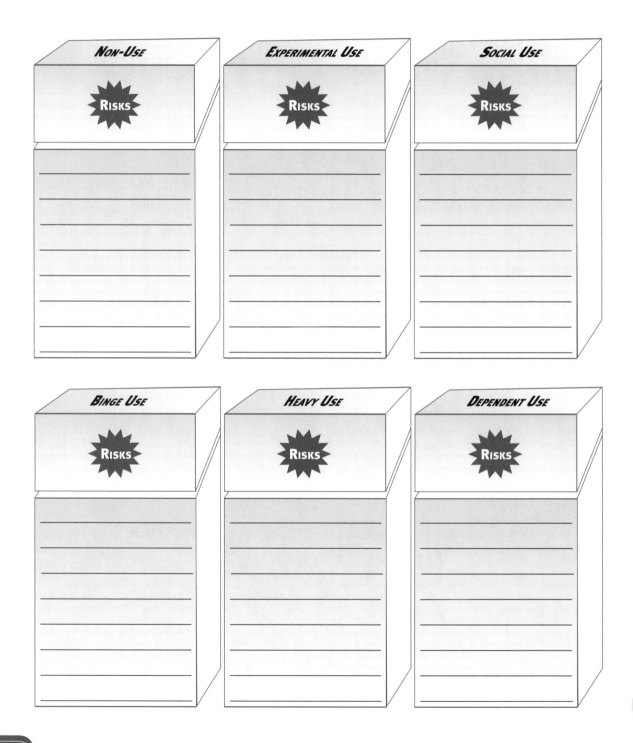

Exercise 5.2

The Effects of Substance Use

Look in the Book
Pages: 244–245, 247–248, 250–253

Many drugs have harmful side effects; damaging a person's brain, lungs, or other vital organs, and affecting a person's judgement and relationships.

Mission: Use the space provided in the table below to briefly identify and describe the physical and/or sociological effects each drug class can have on the body.

Student name: _____

Class/Period: _____

Date: _____

Assessed by: _____

Teacher ☐

Peer ☐

Self ☐

	CANNABIS EXAMPLE:_____	**HALLUCINOGENS** EXAMPLE:_____	**CNS DEPRESSANTS** EXAMPLE:_____	**CNS STIMULANTS** EXAMPLE:_____
EFFECTS ON HEART AND CIRCULATORY SYSTEM				
EFFECTS ON RESPIRATORY SYSTEM				
EFFECTS ON REPRODUCTIVE SYSTEM				
EFFECTS ON CENTRAL NERVOUS SYSTEM (CNS)				
EFFECTS ON DIGESTIVE SYSTEM				
SOCIOLOGICAL EFFECTS (FAMILY, FRIENDS, AND COMMUNITY)				

Drug Dependence

One of the most frequently discussed risks of drug abuse is that of dependence—both physical and psychological. Drug dependence is the continued, compulsive use of a substance.

Mission: Read the case studies below. Identify whether the user is experiencing a drug dependence, either physical or psychological, and think about the advice you'd give them if they asked you for help.

Case study #1 : Darren smokes marijuana before every social occasion and outing that he attends. He finds that it relaxes him, heightens his senses, and helps him combat his shyness and engage in conversations more easily. Without it he feels vulnerable, shy, and awkward. He simply cannot cope in a social situation without the aid of marijuana.

| Does Darren have a physical or psychological drug dependence? |

Rationale: _____

_____

| What advice would you give to Darren? |

_____

_____

Case study #2 : Sunil smokes two packs of cigarettes a day. He has tried to quit but finds that he cannot handle a full day without a cigarette. He gets anxious and hostile, restless and dizzy, and he develops an increase in his appetite. Sunil finds these unpleasant symptoms disappear when he smokes so he slips back into his habit of smoking two packs of cigarettes a day.

| Does Sunil have a physical or psychological drug dependence? |

Rationale: _____

_____

| What advice would you give to Sunil? |

_____

_____

Case study #3 : Natalia's family all enjoy a glass of wine every evening with dinner. In fact, Natalia cannot remember having dinner without having a glass of wine with the meal. Wine always accompanies dinner at Natalia's house, but only one glass each, and only at dinner.

| Does Natalia's family have a physical or psychological drug dependence? |

Rationale: _____

_____

| What advice would you give to Natalia's family? |

_____

_____

Exercise 5.3

Drugs and the Law

Student name:

Class/Period:

Date:

Assessed by:

Teacher ☐

Peer ☐

Self ☐

Knowing the effects of drug use and abuse is important. So too is knowing the law and what consequences a person can face for possession of an illegal drug, or driving under the influence of alcohol.

Mission: Read the following scenarios. Decide whether the individual's actions are legal (L) or illegal (I). Mark your decision in the appropriate column then explain why you think the actions are legal or illegal.

SCENARIO	L	I	RATIONALE
❶ Jameson is stopped by the R.I.D.E. program. The police officer asks Jameson to take a breathalyzer test. His BAC is .09 percent.	☐	☐	_____
❷ Angie is 16 years of age. Her family is celebrating Thanksgiving at home and Angie's mom gives her a glass of wine with dinner.	☐	☐	_____
❸ Vijay brings a joint to school and during the lunch break, he and his friend Alan smoke it.	☐	☐	_____
❹ Tania, who is 19 years old, agrees to buy her 16-year-old sister a pack of cigarettes.	☐	☐	_____
❺ Leroy's uncle grows marijuana. Leroy wants to grow marijuana too, so he takes a plant home and tries to grow it in his room.	☐	☐	_____
❻ The police officer conducting the R.I.D.E. program suspended Kristen's license for 12 hours because her BAC was .06 percent.	☐	☐	_____
❼ Frank is leaving his friend's party at the cottage. He knows he's had too much to drink to drive safely, so Frank decides to borrow his friend's motor boat and go home by water.	☐	☐	_____
❽ Mia and Sharon have just turned 19 years of age. They decide to celebrate by having a picnic lunch, including a bottle of wine, at the public beach.	☐	☐	_____
❾ Carlos is hosting a party. He collects everyone's car keys as they arrive. If anyone has been drinking then Carlos keeps the car keys and calls a taxi for his guest.	☐	☐	_____
❿ It is New Years Eve and Elsa's parents are handing out glasses of champagne. They give a glass of champagne to Elsa's friend Jesse, who is 17 years old.	☐	☐	_____

Kicking Addictions

All substance use at all levels of use presents the potential for problems: an accident, a suspension of one's drivers license, a criminal prosecution. When substance use becomes a substance dependence (an addictive behaviour) outside help is often needed. There are a number of treatment options available.

Mission: Using the space provided below, identify support services available in your community for people needing advice on, or help with, kicking an addiction.

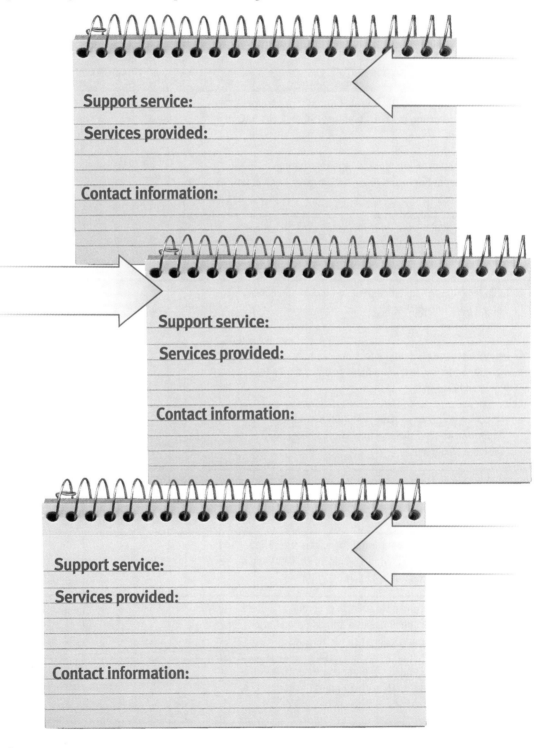

Support service:

Services provided:

Contact information:

Support service:

Services provided:

Contact information:

Support service:

Services provided:

Contact information:

Exercise 5.4

Date Rape Drugs

Look in the Book
Page: 249

Date rape drugs is a term given to drugs such as Rohypnol ®, GHB, and Ketamine, or to any drug that is used to intentionally sedate unsuspecting victims. The victims are then sexually assaulted.

Mission: Before reading page 249 of your *Healthy Active Living* textbook, read the statements below and circle "Agree" or "Disagree," in the left-hand column. After you have completed your assigned reading, go back and read the statements again. Circle "Agree" or "Disagree" in the right-hand column and check to see if your opinion has changed.

Student name:

Class/Period:

Date:

Assessed by:

Teacher ☐

Peer ☐

Self ☐

	BEFORE READING	STATEMENTS	PAGE #	AFTER READING
1.	Agree Disagree	Date rape drugs are used for the purpose of getting someone intoxicated to the point where forced or non-consensual sexual activity can take place with little to no resistance.		Agree Disagree
2.	Agree Disagree	The best way to protect yourself from date rape drugs is to be constantly aware of your surroundings.		Agree Disagree
3.	Agree Disagree	Being under the influence of alcohol can lower your inhibitions and increase the risk of unwanted sexual encounters.		Agree Disagree
4.	Agree Disagree	It's important to know who is pouring your drink or to pour your own drink because some date-rape drugs, like Rohypnol ®, are colourless, tasteless, and odourless.		Agree Disagree
5.	Agree Disagree	If you party with friends you trust, then you are one step closer to protecting yourself from any unwanted sexual encounters.		Agree Disagree
6.	Agree Disagree	There are cases of date rape that go unreported because some date-rape drugs, like Rohypnol ®, can leave the victim with little to no memory of the rape.		Agree Disagree
7.	Agree Disagree	Going home from a party or club with someone you know and trust is an extra measure of precaution to keep yourself safe from unwanted encounters.		Agree Disagree

BEFORE READING		STATEMENTS	PAGE #	AFTER READING
8.	Agree Disagree	The term "Club Drugs" refers to a group of illegal and dangerous substances associated with nightclubs and party venues, and includes the date-rape drugs, Rohypnol ®, GHB, and Ketamine.		Agree Disagree
9.	Agree Disagree	You should immediately throw your drink away if it tastes slightly salty (when it should not) because it could be laced with GHB.		Agree Disagree
10.	Agree Disagree	You should always let your parents or guardians know where you are, who you are with, and what time you will be home.		Agree Disagree
11.	Agree Disagree	It is important to have someone you trust stay with you (or to stay with someone) if you are feeling ill or out of control.		Agree Disagree
12.	Agree Disagree	At high doses, GHB can cause extreme fatigue or unconciousness leaving a victim susceptible to non-consensual sexual activity.		Agree Disagree
13.	Agree Disagree	Taking Ketamine is dangerous because it produces numbness, paralysis, and in high doses, unconsciousness, leaving the user open to assault.		Agree Disagree
14.	Agree Disagree	It is a good idea to have one friend stay sober for the evening to keep an eye out for those who choose to drink.		Agree Disagree
15.	Agree Disagree	Keeping your drink with you at all times prevents anyone from slipping a substance into it with the intent of causing you harm.		Agree Disagree

Now take a closer look at any questions where you changed your mind after reading your *Healthy Active Living* textbook.

What answer surprised you the most?

_____

What did you learn from this exercise?

_____

_____

_____

Unit 5 — Drug Use and Abuse

UNIT 6
Conflict Resolution and Personal Safety

What this unit is about ...

➤ Why will understanding conflict help me to deal with conflict?

➤ What forms of violence have I witnessed in the past, and what can I do to ensure that I don't become a victim or a perpetrator of violence?

Notes:

What Do I Know About Anger Management?

The following exercise should be completed without the use of your textbook.

Mission: Read each statement and indicate whether you think they are "True" or "False."

---

❶ Anger is the most common emotion accompanying conflict. | TRUE ☐ | FALSE ☐

Rationale:

---

❷ Behind most anger is fear. | TRUE ☐ | FALSE ☐

Rationale:

---

❸ Relaxation techniques are one example of an anger-management strategy. | TRUE ☐ | FALSE ☐

Rationale:

---

❹ You can often control your anger once you identify the cause(s). | TRUE ☐ | FALSE ☐

Rationale:

---

❺ You can often avoid conflict situations by taking more responsibility for your actions and behaviour. | TRUE ☐ | FALSE ☐

Rationale:

---

❻ Anger is the only way to effectively handle a conflict. | TRUE ☐ | FALSE ☐

Rationale:

---

❼ Walking away from a conflict means that you are running away from the problem. | TRUE ☐ | FALSE ☐

Rationale:

---

❽ Putting yourself in the other person's shoes is one step to reducing your anger. | TRUE ☐ | FALSE ☐

Rationale:

---

❾ Temporarily removing yourself from a conflict allows you time to cool down and express your anger in ways that are not aggressive or confrontational. | TRUE ☐ | FALSE ☐

Rationale:

---

❿ Anger-management strategies cannot be learned. | TRUE ☐ | FALSE ☐

Rationale:

Conflict

Conflict is a part of life, and it affects everyone. Your reactions and methods of dealing with conflict are important. Understanding the roots of conflict will give you the tools to respond effectively.

Mission: Before reading Chapter 16 of your *Healthy Active Living* textbook, read the statements below and circle "Agree" or "Disagree" in the left-hand column. After you have completed your assigned reading, go back and read the statements again. Circle "Agree" or "Disagree" in the right-hand column and check to see if your opinion has changed.

	BEFORE READING	STATEMENTS	PAGE #	AFTER READING
1.	Agree / Disagree	Conflict can often be constructive.		Agree / Disagree
2.	Agree / Disagree	Negative conflict arises when you don't have the proper tools to deal with conflict.		Agree / Disagree
3.	Agree / Disagree	A conflict is any clash between two or more groups of people.		Agree / Disagree
4.	Agree / Disagree	Conflicts can be resolved more swiftly if you are able to articulate your feelings and possible solutions.		Agree / Disagree
5.	Agree / Disagree	Empathy leads to a greater level of understanding on both sides.		Agree / Disagree
6.	Agree / Disagree	If you are patient and tolerant you are more likely to think before you speak or act.		Agree / Disagree
7.	Agree / Disagree	Conflict-resolution skills can be learned and practised.		Agree / Disagree
8.	Agree / Disagree	Being aggressive is a negative approach to conflict.		Agree / Disagree
9.	Agree / Disagree	Approaching problems from different viewpoints allows you to brainstorm solutions together.		Agree / Disagree
10.	Agree / Disagree	Active listening lets the other person know that you are paying attention and genuinely want to find a solution.		Agree / Disagree

Now take a closer look at any questions where you changed your mind after reading your *Healthy Active Living* textbook.

What answer surprised you the most?

_____

What did you learn from this exercise?

_____

_____

Exercise 6.2

Non-Verbal and Verbal Responses

Look in the Book
Page: 267

Active Listening is a key skill that can not only de-escalate a conflict, but also prevent a conflict from occurring. Active listening lets the other person know that you are paying attention to what they are saying.

Mission: Reflect on what being an active listener entails. Brainstorm words, gestures, or sounds that pertain to active listening and write them in the spaces provided below.

Student name:

Class/Period:

Date:

Assessed by:

Teacher ☐

Peer ☐

Self ☐

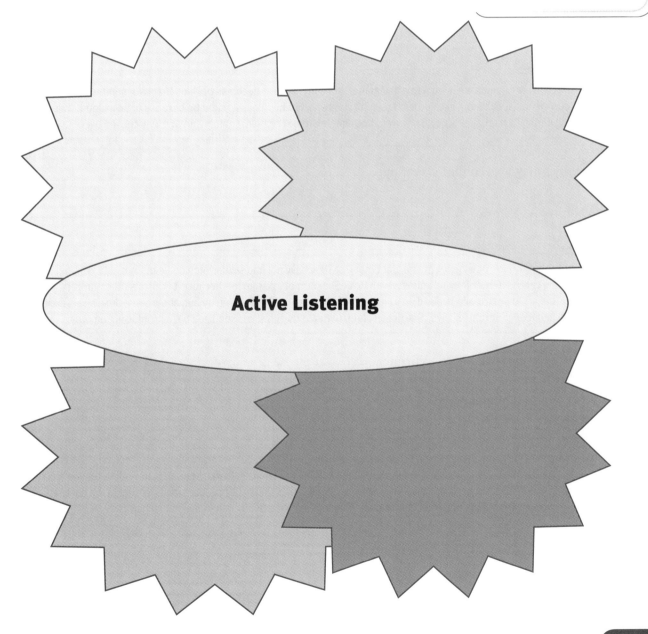

Active Listening

Handling Conflict

Look in the Book
Pages: 264–267

Conflict-resolution skills and abilities can help individuals resolve even the most difficult of conflict situations. It is important to learn how to apply these skills so that workable solutions to conflicts can be achieved.

Mission: Read the case studies below. Identify what type of conflict is occurring and what should be done to resolve it.

An intense soccer game just finished in H&PE class. While walking back to the school gymnasium, Sharon accuses Phillipa of hogging the ball and ignoring their team, which cost them the game. Phillipa accuses Sharon of being lazy and not getting involved in the game to help the team. They begin yelling and some of the team players start taking sides. You think the argument may escalate.

Identify the type of conflict occurring. - - - - - - - - - - - - - - ➤

What should you do? _____

_____

Nate and his three friends are driving to a ball game. While in the car, it becomes obvious that two members of the group are not speaking to each other. Nate isn't sure why, but he thinks it might be because of an incident that occurred during basketball practice. They were both hoping to be the team captain and one was chosen over the other.

Identify the type of conflict occurring. - - - - - - - - - - - - - - ➤

What should Nate do? _____

_____

Augusta and Vijay have been going out for eight months. They have not had sexual intercourse but Augusta is interested in exploring various forms of sexual intimacy with Vijay. She has not told him this because it is against her moral and religious beliefs to be sexually involved with anyone before marriage. She feels guilty but, at the same time, she is excited by these heightened sexual feelings. She doesn't know what to do and she is confused by her conflicting emotions.

Identify the type of conflict occurring. - - - - - - - - - - - - - - ➤

What should Augusta do? _____

_____

Luc arranged a ride home from the high school dance with his friend Tarik, but he hasn't seen him all evening. At the end of the dance, Luc finally finds Tarik out in the high school parking lot. Tarik smells like beer, and Luc notices that Tarik is struggling to walk in a straight line. Luc offers to drive but Tarik insists that he is fine. Luc stands in front of the driver's side door and demands that Tarik hand him the car keys. Tarik tells Luc to back off, step aside, and let him drive.

Identify the type of conflict occurring. - - - - - - - - - - - - - - ➤

What should Luc do? _____

_____

Solving Conflicts

Look in the Book
Page: 266

There are positive and negative approaches to resolving conflict. Following a few basic guidelines when solving a conflict can help you work towards an amicable solution.

Mission: Create a scenario that involves two individuals in a conflict situation. State the problem, the scope of the problem, possible solutions, consequences of each solution, and decide upon the solution that best serves both parties. Your teacher may have you work in pairs for this exercise.

Student name:

Class/Period:

Date:

Assessed by:

Teacher ☐

Peer ☐

Self ☐

State the problem. Be assertive and direct, and avoid personal attacks or laying blame.

_____

_____

_____

_____

Define the scope of the problem and list the areas of agreement and disagreement.

_____

_____

_____

_____

_____

_____

_____

Brainstorm possible solutions; create a list of ways the problem could be solved, without judging the effectiveness of any solution and identify the consequences of each solution.

_____

_____

_____

_____

_____

_____

_____

_____

_____

Discuss and jointly choose the solution that is the most effective for, and acceptable to, both parties

_____

_____

_____

_____

_____

Mediation and Adjudication

Look in the Book

Pages: 270–271

Often two people, or groups of people, find that they cannot resolve a conflict on their own. In these cases, it is useful for both sides to bring in a third party who can help them reach a solution.

Mission: Use the chart below to explore the various ways of achieving third-party conflict resolution. Then list the effects each method of third-party conflict resolution may have on the situation and how they achieve a solution.

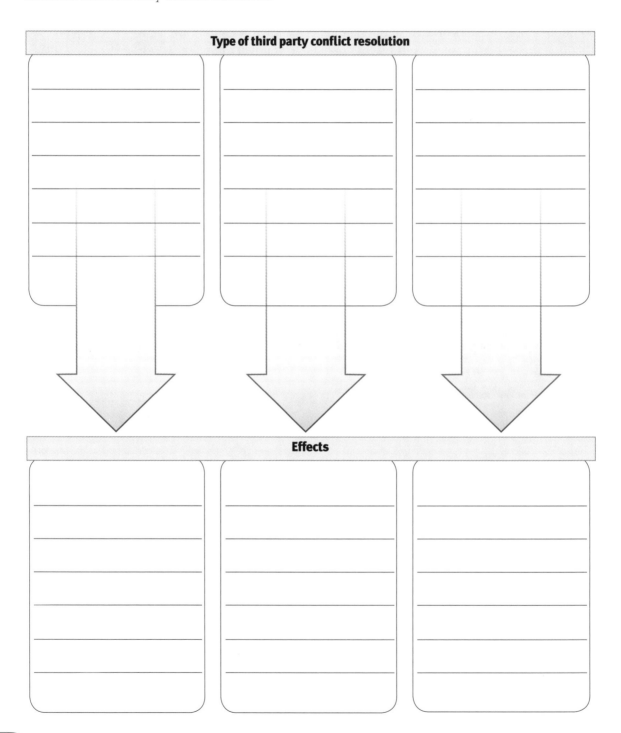

Type of third party conflict resolution

Effects

UNIT 7
Nutrition for Everyday Performance

What this unit is about ...

> What tools can I use to ensure that I am achieving the right nutritional balance for me?

> Why are there nutrition labels on food packages and why do I need to know how to interpret them?

> How does my body image affect my self-esteem and my eating habits?

Notes:

Exercise 7.1

Nutrition for Everyday Performance

The following exercises should be completed without the use of your textbook.

Mission: Read each statement and indicate whether you think they are "True" or "False."

❶ Nutrition is the science behind how your body uses the components of food to grow, maintain, and repair itself. | TRUE ☐ | FALSE ☐

Rationale:

❷ Your body needs more than 50 nutrients on a daily basis in order to function properly. | TRUE ☐ | FALSE ☐

Rationale:

❸ Carbohydrates, proteins, and fats are known as the "energy nutrients." | TRUE ☐ | FALSE ☐

Rationale:

❹ Micronutrients are the essential nutrients that we need in large amounts every day. | TRUE ☐ | FALSE ☐

Rationale:

❺ Vitamins help make bones, proteins, and blood. | TRUE ☐ | FALSE ☐

Rationale:

❻ A calorie is, in fact, a kilocalorie (1000 calories). | TRUE ☐ | FALSE ☐

Rationale:

❼ The Canada Food Guide to Healthy Eating translates Recommended Dietary Allowances of nutrients into actual advice that people can use to plan their food choices on a daily basis. | TRUE ☐ | FALSE ☐

Rationale:

❽ All of the information in the Nutrition Facts table is based on a specific amount of food. | TRUE ☐ | FALSE ☐

Rationale:

❾ There are 15 core nutrients listed on the Nutrition Facts table. | TRUE ☐ | FALSE ☐

Rationale:

❿ Daily values for carbohydrates, total fat, and saturated and trans fat are based on a 2000-calorie diet. | TRUE ☐ | FALSE ☐

Rationale:

Body Image and Self-Esteem

Body image includes how you think others see you, and how you see yourself. How you see yourself plays a vital role in shaping your sense of self-esteem.

Mission: Before reading Chapter 20 of your *Healthy Active Living* textbook, read the statements below and circle "Agree" or "Disagree" in the left-hand column. After you have completed your assigned reading, go back and read the statements again. Circle "Agree" or "Disagree" in the right-hand column and check to see if your opinion has changed.

	BEFORE READING	STATEMENTS	PAGE #	AFTER READING
1.	Agree Disagree	Self-esteem describes how valued or worthy a person feels.		Agree Disagree
2.	Agree Disagree	Being involved in pursuits that are personally rewarding can help you achieve a more rounded view of yourself.		Agree Disagree
3.	Agree Disagree	"The camera never lies."		Agree Disagree
4.	Agree Disagree	Comparing your body to those depicted in the media can leave you feeling dejected and dissatisfied.		Agree Disagree
5.	Agree Disagree	Digital retouching creates unrealistic expectations for an often unsuspecting public.		Agree Disagree
6.	Agree Disagree	Eating disorders are complex illnesses that affect both physical and mental health.		Agree Disagree
7.	Agree Disagree	It is estimated that three percent of women will be affected by eating disorders in their lifetime.		Agree Disagree
8.	Agree Disagree	The best way to achieve a healthy weight is through a combination of healthy eating, regular activity, and taking care of yourself.		Agree Disagree
9.	Agree Disagree	A healthy body image is particularly important for young people.		Agree Disagree
10.	Agree Disagree	Your body is a tool that can help you enjoy and take hold of life's opportunities and challenges.		Agree Disagree

Now take a closer look at any questions where you changed your mind after reading your *Healthy Active Living* textbook.

What answer surprised you the most?

_____

What did you learn from this exercise?

_____

_____

Exercise 7.1   **Unit 7—Nutrition for Everyday Performance**

Exercise 7.2

Total Daily Caloric Need

Look in the Book
Pages: 298–299

No two people are exactly alike when it comes to the amount of calories they need each day. Gender, body size, genetics, age, and physical activity will all influence your Total Daily Caloric Need.

Mission: Using the Harris Benedict formula, calculate your Resting Metabolic Rate (RMR) to estimate your Total Daily Caloric Need.

Student name:

Class/Period:

Date:

Assessed by:

Teacher ☐

Peer ☐

Self ☐

The Harris Benedict Equation:

$66 + (5 \times$ _____ cm) $+ (13.7 \times$ _____ kg) $- (6.8 \times$ _____ yrs) $=$ ☐

height   weight   age

Total Daily Caloric Need:

ACTIVITY FACTOR	CALCULATION	RESULT
If you are sedentary (little to no exercise)	_____ RMR × 1.2	
If you are lightly active (light exercise/sports 1–3 days/week)	_____ RMR × 1.375	
If you are moderately active (moderate exercise/sports 3–5 days/week	_____ RMR × 1.55	
If you are very active (hard exercise/sports 6–7 days/week	_____ RMR × 1.725	
If you are extra active (very hard exercise/sports)	_____ RMR × 1.9	

My Total Daily Caloric Need is - →

It is important that I meet my Total Daily Caloric Need because:

_____

_____

I can improve upon or maintain my daily activity factor by:

_____

_____

By improving or maintaining my activity factor, I not only increase my Total Daily Caloric Need but also improve my:

_____

_____

Canada's Food Guide to Healthy Eating

Look in the Book
Pages: 306–307, 318–319

A diet of balanced, nutritious meals combined with regular physical activity, enables you to achieve and maintain a healthy body weight, have more energy, and enjoy better overall health. When eating, try to limit foods and beverages that are high in calories, fat, sugar, and salt.

Mission: Using the chart below, insert the number of servings you should have each day, according to *Canada's Food Guide* and record your actual food choices and servings by shading in the symbols.

FOOD GROUP	RNS*	NUMBER OF SERVINGS I CONSUMED		
		Day One	Day Two	Day Three
Vegetables and Fruit		□□□□□□ □□□□□□	□□□□□□ □□□□□□	□□□□□□ □□□□□□
Grain Products		□□□□□□ □□□□□□	□□□□□□ □□□□□□	□□□□□□ □□□□□□
Milk and Alternatives		□□□□□	□□□□□	□□□□□
Meat and Alternatives		□□□□	□□□□	□□□□
Other		◇◇◇◇◇	◇◇◇◇◇	◇◇◇◇◇

* Recommended Number of Servings

Did you eat a variety of foods from all of the food groups? ------------→ ▢

In what food group did you have the most difficulty meeting the recommended servings? ------------------------------→ ▢

Did your food consumption meet your energy needs for daily activities? ----------------------------→ ▢

How will following the recommended number of servings combined with regular physical activity impact your Total Daily Caloric Need? ------→ ▢

Rationale: _____

_____

Understanding % Daily Value

The % Daily Value is based on the recommended daily intakes for each nutrient listed on the Nutrition Facts table. It tells you how much or how little of a nutrient is contained in a particular food item (portion size) in relation to what should be taken in on a daily basis.

Student name:

Class/Period:

Date:

Assessed by:

Teacher ☐

Peer ☐

Self ☐

Choose any food item that you eat on a daily basis. Cut out the Nutrition Facts table from the food package and paste it in the space provided below. Record the main ingredients in this food item. Answer the questions that follow.

Nutrition Label	List of Ingredients

What is the portion size listed on the label (to which the nutritional information relates)? - - - - - - - - - - - - - - - - - →

Record the percentage of your daily recommended intake (%DV) of fats, sodium, carbohydrates, and fibre that you will receive from this portion size. - - - - - - - - - - →

fats ☐ sodium ☐

carbohydrates ☐ fibre ☐

How would you personally rate this food item on a scale of 1–10 (10 being the most nutritious)? - - - - - - - - - - - - - →

Rationale: _____

_____

Nutrition and Healthy Eating

Achieving the right nutritional balance is key to maintaining a healthy body weight and enjoying better overall health.

Mission: You should now have a solid understanding of your Total Daily Caloric Need, nutritional needs, and how to achieve and maintain a healthy, well-balanced diet. Using the knowledge you have gained, create a nutritious menu that includes breakfast, lunch, dinner, and snacks, and be sure to include the serving portions for each item of food listed on the menu.

Today's Special

Breakfast

Snack

Lunch

Snack

Dinner

Snack

Exercise 7.4

Canada's Physical Activity Guide to Healthy Active Living

Student name:

Class/Period:

Date:

Assessed by:

Teacher ☐

Peer ☐

Self ☐

Increasing the amount of time you spend being physically active is not as difficult as you think. Get up, get out, and get active!

Mission: For a period of seven days, implement the three main types of physical activities, as laid out by the *Physical Activity Guide*: aerobic, flexibility, and strengthening. Record the type of activity you did, and include the intensity, duration, and time of day you performed each activity in the table below.

DAY	AEROBIC ACTIVITIES (TYPE, INTENSITY, DURATION, TIME)	FLEXIBILITY ACTIVITIES (TYPE, INTENSITY, DURATION, TIME)	STRENGTHENING ACTIVITIES (TYPE, INTENSITY, DURATION, TIME)
MONDAY			
TUESDAY			
WEDNESDAY			
THURSDAY			
FRIDAY			
SATURDAY			
SUNDAY			

Eating Well and Being Active

The most difficult thing about leading a healthy active lifestyle is recognizing and breaking the bad habits that you may have been predisposed to over the years.

Mission: Now that you have been guided through the steps to achieving a healthy active lifestyle, take a moment to reflect on the impact nutrition and physical activity are having on your overall health. Complete the sentences below with honesty and clarity.

I find I have more energy throughout the day because _____
_____

I handle stress better because _____
_____

Instead of snacking on potato chips, pop, or candies I am choosing healthier substitutes such as
_____

I have noticed that eating well-balanced, nutritious meals has _____
_____

The physical activity that I enjoy the most is _____
_____

I enjoy this activity because _____
_____

I am incorporating a total of _____ minutes a day of physical activity. The benefits that I am feeling are _____

I am comfortable within my body because _____
_____

Now that I am aware of the importance of nutrition and how it affects my physical and emotional health I intend to _____
_____
_____
_____

Exercise 7.5

Factors that Influence Body Image

Body image is dynamic. **How you see yourself changes over time due to various influential factors, such as the media, your family, and your friends. Media communications especially often try to enforce an "ideal" body type.**

Student name:
_____

Class/Period:
_____
Date:
_____
Assessed by:

Teacher ☐
Peer ☐
Self ☐

Mission: Take a popular magazine (Cosmo Girl, Seventeen, Teen Trend, Men's Health) and study five advertisements. List them, and answer the following questions.

List of advertisements:

_____ _____

_____ _____

1. Who do you think the advertisements are targeting?

_____

_____

2. What are the similarities and differences between the advertisements?

Similarities: Differences:

_____ _____   _____ _____

_____ _____   _____ _____

3. Do the advertisements provide a positive and realistic representation of girls/boys, women/men? - - - - →

Rationale: _____

_____

4. Do you think these advertisements will affect a reader's perception of body image? - - - - →

Rationale: _____

_____

5. List the ways that each advertisement may have been digitally altered.

_____

_____

Create an Advertisement

Each day we are exposed to hundreds of advertisements featuring "picture perfect" bodies. We respond by comparing ourselves to the images that we see.

Mission: In the space provided below, draw or paste in your own advertisement. Be mindful of what you just studied. Consider your target audience, the appearance of an average Canadian, and take into account a healthy body image and a healthy sense of self-esteem. Also be sensitive to de-humanizing your advertisement.

Eating Disorders

Look in the Book
Pages: 328–329

Eating disorders are complex and life-threatening illnesses that negatively impact every aspect of an individual's life.

Mission: Read the case studies below and answer the following questions.

Student name:

Class/Period:

Date:

Assessed by:

Teacher ☐

Peer ☐

Self ☐

Case study #1

Laticia is 172 cm tall and weighs 55 kg. She is trying to lose 7 kg so that she can look as thin as the models in fashion magazines. Laticia has a routine of morning jogging and evening cycling. She limits her breakfast to a glass of juice; she skips lunch; and at dinner she eats either a cup of yogourt and a piece of fruit or a salad. When she feels hungry throughout the day she allows herself water only.

Is Laticia making a healthy choice by eating a small amount of food once a day, and performing vigorous exercises? ----------➔

Rationale: _____

_____

Does Laticia have an eating disorder, and if so, what eating disorder does Laticia suffer from? ----------➔

Rationale: _____

_____

Case study #2

Jackie has always been self-conscious about her size, standing at 165 cm tall and weighing 72.5 kg. She has tried various diets and nothing seems to work in getting her weight down. When she diets, she craves salty, greasy foods so much that she often ends up eating them in excess—a large bowl of buttered popcorn, a couple of cheeseburgers, etc.—then purging immediately afterward.

How is Jackie's eating habit affecting her physical and emotional health? ----------➔

Rationale: _____

_____

Does Jackie have an eating disorder, and if so, what eating disorder does Jackie suffer from? ----------➔

Rationale: _____

_____

Getting Help

With so much societal pressure to look a certain way physically and be "perfect," some people find it very difficult to maintain their sense of self-worth and require specialized assistance to help them overcome exceptionally low self-esteem, unhealthy eating habits, or depression.

Mission: Using the space provided below, identify support services available in your community for people needing advice on, or help with, creating and maintaining a healthy body image.

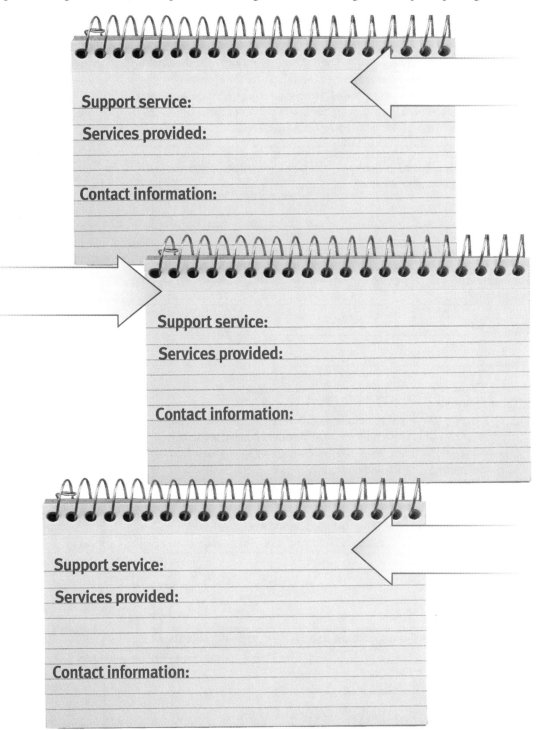

Support service:

Services provided:

Contact information:

Support service:

Services provided:

Contact information:

Support service:

Services provided:

Contact information:

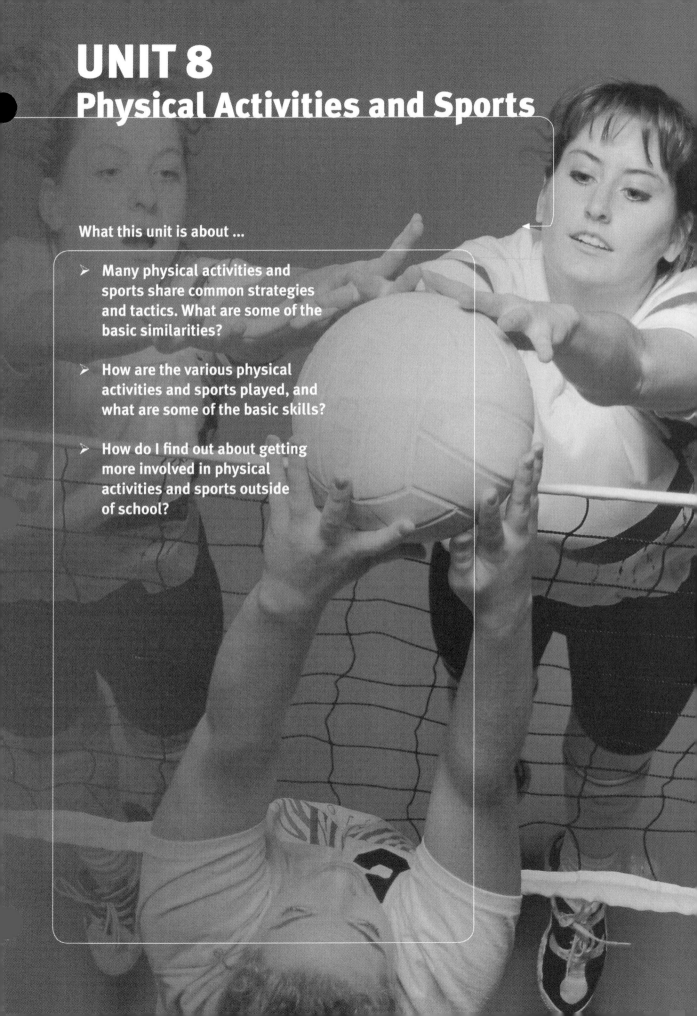

UNIT 8
Physical Activities and Sports

What this unit is about ...

➢ Many physical activities and sports share common strategies and tactics. What are some of the basic similarities?

➢ How are the various physical activities and sports played, and what are some of the basic skills?

➢ How do I find out about getting more involved in physical activities and sports outside of school?

Notes:

Exercise 8.1

Invasion/Territory Games

Look in the Book
Page: 337

Invasion/territory games are some of the most common games that we play. They include sports such as soccer, basketball, ultimate, ice hockey, field hockey, rugby, football, and lacrosse, just to mention a few.

Student name:	
Class/Period:	
Date:	
Assessed by:	
Teacher	☐
Peer	☐
Self	☐

Strategies and Tactics

Mission: Complete the chart below outlining the general strategies and tactics that are used in invasion/territory games. For each strategy and tactical situation, provide sport-specific examples.

STRATEGIES AND TACTICS ON OFFENCE
Overall strategy:
_____
_____
_____
_____
Sport-Specific strategy:
_____
_____
_____
_____

STRATEGIES AND TACTICS ON DEFENCE
Overall strategy:
_____
_____
_____
_____
Sport-Specific strategy:
_____
_____
_____
_____

Phases of a Skill

Mission: Choose a skill from one of the invasion/territory games covered in this chapter. Identify some key points involved in the preparation, execution, and follow-through of this skill and record them on the chart below. Use the "Yes" and "No" columns for self-evaluation, or evaluation by a peer or teacher.

SPORT	NAME		
	SKILL	YES	NO
Preparation		☐	☐
		☐	☐
		☐	☐
		☐	☐
		☐	☐
		☐	☐
		☐	☐
		☐	☐
Execution		☐	☐
		☐	☐
		☐	☐
		☐	☐
		☐	☐
		☐	☐
		☐	☐
		☐	☐
Follow-Through		☐	☐
		☐	☐
		☐	☐
		☐	☐
		☐	☐
		☐	☐
		☐	☐
		☐	☐

Exercise 8.2

Net/Wall Games

Look in the Book
Page: 371

Net/wall games are popular sports that many Canadians enjoy playing. They include sports such as volleyball, badminton, tennis, table tennis, squash, racquetball, and handball.

Strategies and Tactics

Mission: Complete the chart below outlining the general strategies and tactics that are used in net/wall games. For each strategy and tactical situation, provide sport-specific examples.

Student name:

_____

Class/Period:

Date:

Assessed by:

Teacher ☐

Peer ☐

Self ☐

STRATEGIES AND TACTICS ON OFFENCE

Overall strategy:

_____

_____

_____

_____

_____

Sport-Specific strategy:

_____

_____

_____

_____

_____

STRATEGIES AND TACTICS ON DEFENCE

Overall strategy:

_____

_____

_____

_____

_____

Sport-Specific strategy:

_____

_____

_____

_____

_____

Phases of a Skill

Mission: Choose a skill from one of the net/wall games covered in this chapter. Identify some key points involved in the preparation, execution, and follow-through of this skill and record them on the chart below. Use the "Yes" and "No" columns for self-evaluation, or evaluation by a peer or teacher.

SPORT	NAME		
	SKILL	YES	NO
Preparation		☐	☐
		☐	☐
		☐	☐
		☐	☐
		☐	☐
		☐	☐
		☐	☐
		☐	☐
Execution		☐	☐
		☐	☐
		☐	☐
		☐	☐
		☐	☐
		☐	☐
		☐	☐
		☐	☐
Follow-Through		☐	☐
		☐	☐
		☐	☐
		☐	☐
		☐	☐
		☐	☐
		☐	☐
		☐	☐

Striking/Fielding Games

Look in the Book
Page: 389

In striking/fielding games, such as baseball, softball, and cricket, the defensive team delivers the ball to a player on the offensive team. The offensive player attempts to strike the ball and score by running between safe areas, or reaching a safe area without the ball being caught.

Student name: _____

Class/Period: _____

Date: _____

Assessed by:

Teacher ☐

Peer ☐

Self ☐

Strategies and Tactics

Mission: Complete the chart below outlining the general strategies and tactics that are used in striking/fielding games. For each strategy and tactical situation, provide sport-specific examples.

STRATEGIES AND TACTICS ON OFFENCE	STRATEGIES AND TACTICS ON DEFENCE
Overall strategy:	Overall strategy:
Sport-Specific strategy:	Sport-Specific strategy:

Phases of a Skill

Mission: Choose a skill from one of the striking/fielding games covered in this chapter. Identify some key points involved in the preparation, execution, and follow-through of this skill and record them on the chart below. Use the "Yes" and "No" columns for self-evaluation, or evaluation by a peer or teacher.

SPORT	NAME		
	SKILL	YES	NO
Preparation		☐	☐
		☐	☐
		☐	☐
		☐	☐
		☐	☐
		☐	☐
		☐	☐
		☐	☐
Execution		☐	☐
		☐	☐
		☐	☐
		☐	☐
		☐	☐
		☐	☐
		☐	☐
		☐	☐
Follow-Through		☐	☐
		☐	☐
		☐	☐
		☐	☐
		☐	☐
		☐	☐
		☐	☐
		☐	☐

Exercise 8.4

Target Games

The two target games discussed in this unit—curling and golf—are both very popular sporting activities. Other target games include bowling, archery, billiards, bocce, croquet, darts, horseshoe pitching, shuffleboard, and lawn bowling.

Student name:

Class/Period:

Date:

Assessed by:

Teacher ☐

Peer ☐

Self ☐

Strategies and Tactics

Mission: Complete the chart below outlining the general strategies and tactics that are used in target games. For each strategy and tactical situation, provide sport-specific examples.

STRATEGIES AND TACTICS ON OFFENCE	STRATEGIES AND TACTICS ON DEFENCE
Overall strategy:	Overall strategy:
Sport-Specific strategy:	Sport-Specific strategy:

Phases of a Skill

Mission: Choose a skill from one of the target games covered in this chapter. Identify some key points involved in the preparation, execution, and follow-through of this skill and record them on the chart below. Use the "Yes" and "No" columns for self-evaluation, or evaluation by a peer or teacher.

SPORT	NAME		
	SKILL	YES	NO
Preparation		☐	☐
		☐	☐
		☐	☐
		☐	☐
		☐	☐
		☐	☐
		☐	☐
		☐	☐
Execution		☐	☐
		☐	☐
		☐	☐
		☐	☐
		☐	☐
		☐	☐
		☐	☐
		☐	☐
Follow-Through		☐	☐
		☐	☐
		☐	☐
		☐	☐
		☐	☐
		☐	☐
		☐	☐
		☐	☐

Notes:

Notes:

Notes:

Notes:

no trim

L.R.

52×205